Stanier Locomotives

Stanier Locomotives

A Pictorial History by Brian Haresnape

LONDON

IAN ALLAN LTD

Previous Page: 'Princess Coronation' Pacific No 46245 *City of London* is seen on the turntable at Crewe North, with railtour headboard./*J.R. Carter*

Below: Stanier's classic mixed-traffic design, the 'Black Five' was to be found virtually all over the LMSR system. No 45258 was photographed in the lined black livery of BR days, with a freight at the top of Chequerbent Bank, near Bolton./*J.R. Carter*

First published 1970
This edition 1981

ISBN 0 7110 1098 6

© Brian Haresnape 1970, 1981

Published by Ian Allan Ltd, Shepperton, Surrey,
and printed by Ian Allan Printing Ltd at their
works at Coombelands in Runnymede, England.

Below: 'Jubilee' class 4-6-0s Nos 45675 *Hardy* and 45562
Alberta at Carnforth on 17 June 1967./*P. Claxton*

Contents

Foreword

There are some names which will remain immortal in the 160 year saga of steam locomotion, and amongst these will stand that of William Arthur Stanier.

No theoretician, but a born mechanic; no autocrat, but a human and kindly man, he did not himself invent anything, and yet a Stanier locomotive was unmistakable to all students of steam. His fame rested on the bold and imaginative manner in which he re-stocked the LMSR, on the harmonious way in which he combined two opposed schools of locomotive design, and on the influence his work had upon his followers down to the last days of steam.

The author of this pictorial survey has brought understanding and evident enjoyment to the congenial task of relating something about each of the different designs for which Stanier was reponsible, and in selecting a range of illustrations which will make these vanished engines re-live for all those who knew and loved them in their heyday.

E. S. Cox

Introduction

Few of us who grew up during the years when the locomotives described in this work were the mainstay of the LMSR motive power fleet, could have foreseen the astonishingly swift decline and fall of steam power on British Railways. To us these rugged and powerful workhorses were a part of our everyday life—our environment—and the sights and sounds of steam formed a constant backcloth to our activities.

We could not visualise—nor, I suppose, did we wish to—the spectacle of Shap Fell without that relentless battle for adhesion which sent sounds echoing far across the bleak hillsides to mingle with the bleat of sheep and the cry of the curlews, and dark powerful exhausts high into the sky overhead. To us, such railway centres as Crewe, Derby or Carlisle were the palaces of steam, and many were the pilgrimages we made. In the postwar era, when 'spotting' was most prolific, we took for granted those regular gatherings of enthusiasts on platforms and linesides; complete with ABCs, notebooks and sandwiches. Steam, and in particular steam in action, roused us and enthralled us as no diesel or electric can do today.

On the LMSR it was the locomotives of Sir William Stanier which represented the character of that great railway during its finest years, and somehow the deep mellow tone of the Caledonian bass siren, which Stanier adopted in place of the usual high-pitched locomotive whistle, seemed to play an important part in the proceedings. Whether heard from afar, across the landscape, or in the confines of an industrial yard or large station, the Stanier siren evoked the same image; one of sturdy modern locomotives, efficiently working the trains of Britain's largest railway system.

When W. A. Stanier accepted the post of Chief Mechanical Engineer of the London Midland and Scottish Railway, commencing on 1 January, 1932, he also accepted a personal challenge of considerable proportions. His career, until then, had been influenced by the strong traditions and progressive policies which had been established by G. J. Churchward at Swindon, for the Great Western Railway. In the early years of this century, Churchward had developed a fleet of standard locomotive types with modern design features. The Swindon designs were so good, in fact, that they remained the basis for all subsequent development on the GWR, and C. B. Collett (who succeeded Churchward as CME), continued with a steady policy of refinement and improvement that must have seemed like second nature to him.

In contrast, when Stanier moved from Swindon (where he had been Collett's Principal Assistant, and a leading member of an established and brilliant team), to the LMSR, he was faced with a situation far less settled. I do not need to repeat here the story of the early years on the LMSR, when Fowler was in charge at Derby—culminating as it did with the extraordinary affair of the design and construction of the 'Royal Scot' class—as this has been told both ably and often. The important point is, that after a period of frustration and confusion, the arrival of Stanier must have represented a heaven-sent opportunity to 'get down to brass tacks'. There were certainly some keen and devoted staff in the drawing offices; all they needed was a clear directive.

On the other hand, Stanier came to a railway which had already developed the organisation of locomotive repairs to a high degree (partly under the guidance of Beames), and had cut down time in the workshops to a level not attained by any other company. All that was still lacking was an appreciation of the value of fine and accurate workmanship, and this was the very quality which Stanier (by virtue of both his instinct and his Swindon training) was able to graft onto existing LMSR practices, to produce overall maintenance standards unsurpassed anywhere in the country.

The earliest ideas of the Stanier era were formed around the introduction of a new range of boilers and with only limited new construction of locomotives, in particular a Pacific design for express passenger work. This policy was presumably a result of Stanier's GWR experience, where many of the engines absorbed at the Grouping were subsequently reboilered and 'Swindonised'. It was only when mechanical performance was investigated and many shortcomings were exposed that Stanier decided upon a 'scrap and build' policy instead.

Obviously Stanier was faced with some unpleasant tasks, not least in the field of human relationships, and the early days must have been tense indeed for him, as he established both his own technical beliefs and his personality in 'foreign' surroundings.

In view of this, the appearance of his first important locomotive, the Pacific No 6200 *The Princess Royal,* just 17 months after he had taken

office, is all the more remarkable. Here at last was the heavy express power—comparable to that on the rival LNER—to work the heavy Anglo-Scottish expresses. But this was just the beginning of what might justifiably be called a motive power revolution. The greatest need was for mixed-traffic power, and for locomotives capable of working over most parts of the LMSR system. Designs were completed for 4-6-0s (both 2- and 3-cylinder versions), for 2-6-4Ts, 2-6-2Ts, and a heavy freight 2-8-0. These began to emerge in 1934/5, by which time considerable experience had been gained with the prototype Pacifics, and with a batch of 40 2-6-0s, which had been constructed at Crewe.

The most important early lessons learned were that tube proportions and ratios required a much closer study than had previously been accorded to them, and that Swindon style low-degree superheat did not come up to expectations in LMSR operating conditions. Experience with Nos 6200/1 soon showed the need for second thoughts on these features, and a series of modifications (revising the tube arrangements and enlarging superheaters) took place in attempts to improve steaming. Similar troubles arose with the early batches of domeless,

low-degree superheat boilers, particularly on the three cylinder 4-6-0 engines and determined efforts to improve matters soon produced results, which were applied to other boiler types in turn. Once Stanier had shaken off some of his preconceived Swindon ideas the way was clear for experiment—albeit on a somewhat hit-and-miss basis, as there were no testing-plant facilities comparable to those available in later years. Nevertheless, improvements in boiler design and draughting were soon forthcoming, and the way was clear for production of a range of highly satisfactory standard locomotive designs. By the end of 1935 there were 325 Stanier locomotives in service, whilst by the end of 1939 no less than 1,225 were in service, and a wholesale slaughter of pre-Grouping types had taken place.

Whilst on the subject of boiler design, I would mention that in the following pages I have attempted to portray the main changes and improvements that took place with each class. But a few general words here would not be at all out of place. All the Stanier designs except No 6170 *British Legion* and the 'Coronation' class Pacifics, started life with domeless boilers, which were associated with two row (low-degree) superheaters. Except in the case of the first 10 2-6-0s (see Section 2), the safety valves were on the firebox, and the small dome cover amidships in fact housed the top feed valves. No Stanier engine had a combined dome and top feed—

despite frequent references to such a feature in the enthusiast press. As soon as it was found to be desirable to introduce a steam dome on top of the taper boiler the top feed was placed separately just ahead of it in a semi-cylindrical casing. A boiler variation which is not readily discernible from study of photographs, should also be mentioned. The earliest Stanier engines had vertical firebox throatplates and long boiler barrel and tubes. To obtain better proportions, later boilers of the tender classes had sloping throatplates which provided a firebox longer in the upper part, to give a better combustion volume, and tubes 1ft shorter than on the originals, which in conjunction with smaller diameter tubes permitted large free area, so important for lively steam production.

The type of boiler fitted can be discerned from illustrations of Stanier locomotives by the presence or absence of a dome; except in the case of the 3-cylinder 4-6-0s, where 108 out of 113 boilers originally built domeless were altered. In side views of these engines the position of the joint between the barrel and firebox, relative to the nearby splasher—or the number of washout plugs on the side of the firebox, there being one more on sloping throatplate boilers—shows which type was fitted. The boilers for tank engines retained the vertical throatplate, but by sloping the backplate a larger grate area was obtained. In photographs the difference is evident by the presence of the dome on the later boilers, except in the case of 2-6-2T Nos 121—144, which were domeless and these

Left: 'Princess Royal' Pacific No 46210 *Lady Patricia* nearing Grayrigg in April 1959 with a Liverpool to Glasgow train./*W.J.V. Anderson*

Above: Specially finished in a livery of glossy black and chromium plated fittings, in honour of the Silver Jubilee of King George V, Stanier 'Jubilee' class 4-6-0 No 5552 *Silver Jubilee* is seen here at Watford South on 22 July 1939, at the head of an up Blackpool and Fylde Coast express./*E.R. Wethersett*

boilers were confined to that particular batch.

A change in the format of this revised edition concerns the presentation of the principal dimensions, including boiler details. As individual batches, or indeed individual locomotives varied, both when new and during their lives, I have decided to attach *typical* dimensions for each class in a separate box together with the locomotive diagram. Some specific boiler details are still included in the text and captions, where of historical importance.

The taper boiler, with separate dome and top feed, became the hallmark of a Stanier locomotive, along with a good looking chimney and generally neat appearance. There was no embellishment of the type favoured by Swindon, of copper or brass, but the workmanship was good and the designs bore considerable evidence that both functional and aesthetic aspects had received careful attention at the drawing board stage. One could eulogise for hours on, for example, the magnificent 'Coronation' Pacifics or the sturdy 'Black Fives', but I would rather that the pictures for the most part spoke for themselves. Aesthetically, I consider that all Stanier locomotives were well proportioned and well detailed, with the exception of his early 2-6-0 design and his small 2-6-2T. (Is it pure coincidence that these two types proved to be the least satisfactory in service, I wonder?). The term handsome is certainly appropriate to all his express passenger engines, whilst the transformation Stanier brought about when he rebuilt the Fowler 'Royal Scots' was striking indeed.

It is not my intention to dwell upon details of Stanier's personal career, as this aspect has already been excellently portrayed in two biographies,* whilst the background story to the design and development of his locomotives has also been brilliantly essayed.† The object of this present work is to present, in pictorial format, the general story of the Stanier engines. I hope that many fond memories will be revived by the illustrations, and that at the same time, a clearer picture of their development and operation will present itself to the reader. Although the emphasis is upon the visual, rather than the purely technical aspects of Stanier's locomotives, I have not considered it necessary to give exhaustive details of the livery changes and variations which took place (although a few special liveries are mentioned as a matter of

general interest), as this aspect has also been comprehensively described in a recent book. ‡ Neither have I included details of specific performances by locomotives, either in everyday service or on test runs, as this aspect has been most fully chronicled over the years by such noted experts as Cecil J. Allen and O. S. Nock. Accidents involving Stanier locomotives are mentioned only where these unfortunate tragedies tell any relevant story concerning design.

Two locomotive designs, often attributed to Stanier, are not described. I refer of course to the small 0-4-0ST and the 0-4-4T. The saddletank was a pure Kitson industrial design, ordered in a form to suit the needs of the LMSR, and had no Stanier influence at all. It is interesting to find that Crewe was to have built these five engines at a total cost of £12,220 but in July 1932 the order was

* William Stanier. *A biography by O. S. Nock. Ian Allan Ltd. and* Master Builders of Steam. *H. A. V Bulleid. Ian Allan Ltd.* †Locomotive Panorama *(2 Vols.). E. S. Cox. Ian Allan Ltd.*

‡ Locomotive Liveries of the LMS, *D. Jenkinson, Roundhouse Books Ian Allan Ltd.*

Left: Streamlined 'Princess Coronation' Pacific No 6223 *Princess Alice* in Crewe station at the head of a West of England train. Note the 'winged' oil lamp./*E. Treacy*

Above: In BR blue livery 'Princess Coronation' Pacific No 46250 *City of Lichfield* makes a superb picture at the head of the 'Royal Scot' express climbing Beattock, with rear end banking assistance./*E. Treacy*

transferred to Kitson, who quoted £7,379. The 0-4-4T was typical of the Fowler era and had been authorised for construction in the 1931 programme, when E. J. H. Lemon was CME, and Stanier was in no way responsible ; although someone later assumed that he would expect it to have a stovepipe chimney!

Were one to credit these designs to Stanier, it would be equally logical to say that the batches of Fowler 0-6-0s produced as late as 1937-41 were also Stanier types! Likewise, the 2-6-0 (see page 16), and 2-6-4T designs for the LMSR-operated Northern Counties Committee line, in Northern Ireland, were basically Fowler engines, with parallel boilers. In fact, on the 2-6-0, the boiler, cylinders, valve gear and all details were almost identical with the LMSR Fowler 2-6-4Ts (although the shape of the grate was different), but with the coupled wheels increased to 6ft diameter.

Stanier's influence upon the final years of steam locomotive design in this country was considerable. The team which worked so well to produce his LMSR standard types was destined to continue along a similar path, culminating with the BR standard designs of 1951. When, in 1942, Stanier was appointed as a scientific advisor for the Ministry of Production, he ceased to take an active part in the locomotive affairs of the LMSR, although he remained as a consultant. C. E. Fairburn was appointed as acting CME until late in 1944 when Stanier resigned in order to devote himself fully to his wartime post. But the resignation of Stanier—sad blow though it undoubtedly was to the LMSR—did not mean the end of the Stanier policy. Fairburn, and finally, H.

Left: Final form of the 'Princess Coronation' Pacifics; minus streamlining. No 46225 *Duchess of Gloucester,* photographed at Winwick on a Crewe–Carlisle parcels train, August 1964. The yellow stripe on the cabside denoted that the engine was not permitted to operate under electrified catenary south of Crewe./*J.R. Carter*

Below: The standard cab layout of Stanier's locomotives was much appreciated by the enginemen. Visibility was good, and comfortable tip-up seats were provided. Illustrated is the cab of No 6220 *Coronation (alias* 6229) as specially prepared for the 1939 American Tour./*BR*

Below right: The first Stanier design to appear was something of a mixture of practices, with a Swindon-influenced taper boiler mounted upon frames of Horwich origin, and coupled to a Derby-type tender. The safety valves were at first located on the boiler barrel, in a dome-shaped casing (initially this was to have been a GWR-type bonnet as shown on page 27) and this feature is well evident in this view of No 13254 on a pw works train at Penrith, in June 1935./*H.C. Casserley*

G. Ivatt, continued to develop his standard types, bringing in modifications only when the changed operating conditions of the immediate postwar years dictated that increased emphasis must be placed upon labour-saving maintenance and servicing, to reduce costs.

Since publication of the first edition of this book in 1970 a drawing has come to light (reproduced on page 17) which shows the way Stanier's team were thinking back in 1942. In the midst of war all available locomotive building capacity was geared to heavy freight and mixed-traffic engines, but Stanier's draughtsmen apparently had time enough to contemplate the types of locomotives that may be required with a return to peacetime conditions. As the drawing shows, two large new types, with eight-wheeled tenders and mechanical stokers were planned. One was basically a super 'Princess Coronation' with a 4-6-4 wheel arrangement and 300psi boiler pressure. This would have had a streamlined outer-casing and was intended for the Anglo-Scottish services. The other was an impressive 4-8-4 large freight locomotive which, it is believed, would have been employed upon fast container trains, of a concept not dissimilar to todays' 'Freightliners'. Both designs would probably have featured bar frames.

No greater tribute can be formed to the soundness of design and construction of the locomotives of William Stanier, than that examples survived in use right up to the final day of steam operation on British Railways, and that they outlived many engines introduced in later days. Recognition of his own personality and achievements included Knighthood in 1943, and election as a Fellow of The Royal Society in 1944.

Throughout the preparation of this work—which has in itself proved a most enjoyable task—I have had the invaluable help of two men, and I wish to place on record my sincere thanks for all the assistance and advice they have so willingly given. My thanks, therefore, to E. S. Cox (whose letters are as informative and enjoyable as the excellent books he has written), for reading the manuscript and for advice upon the technical details; and to Alec Swain for so patiently collecting a vast quantity of references and data, which has proved invaluable in sorting out the overall story. For this present edition I am deeply indebted to Peter Rowledge, for checking the manuscript against his own comprehensive files on Stanier's locomotives. Much new light has been shed upon the 8F 2-8-0s in particular by his researches, and this and other material is now included in the revised text and illustrations. For the new section devoted to the preserved

engines I am grateful to John Edgington for providing much data. Many people, from many parts of the world have written to me about Stanier and his locomotives, and I would like to take this opportunity to express my thanks to all of them for the interest they have shown.

Finally I would also like to thank the following for their help in supplying information or photographs: J. R. Carter; H. C. Casserley; R. G. Jarvis; E. J. Jones; D. Jenkinson; P. M. Kalla-Bishop; S. C. Nash and P. Ransome-Wallis. The line drawings are reproduced by courtesy of the *Railway Gazette* and the National Railway Museum.

Author's Note to this new Edition
In the decade since *Stanier Locomotives* was first published the locomotive preservation movement has been firmly established. It seems appropriate that this historical account should be brought up-to-date to include the engines which have been saved from the scrapyards and which, in a number of cases, are once again in full working order. I have added a new section, at the end of the book describing these preserved engines. There is also a new appendix giving

Above: Although the chimney, top feed and tender show Stanier influence, the overall design of the Northern Counties Committee 2-6-0s (and the basically similar 2-6-4Ts) was based upon the Fowler 2300 series 2-6-4Ts of the LMSR. Stanier did not interfere with the design. No 102 is shown on Royal Train duty./*UTA*

brief details of the LMSR diesel shunting locomotives. I have taken the opportunity to revise the text and illustrations, as it has been necessary for technical reasons to reset the book completely to suit today's printing methods. Some of the original photographs have gone missing over the years, whilst some others have become too familiar, due to repeated use in other books by other authors. I have replaced these wherever possible by similar but less well known illustrations, and I have also added a number of new ones which have only recently come to light. Some small changes to the basic presentation and layout have been made, with the reader in mind, in particular by the segregation of principal dimensions from the text.

Brian Haresnape, FRSA, NDD,
Dorking, Surrey
May 1980

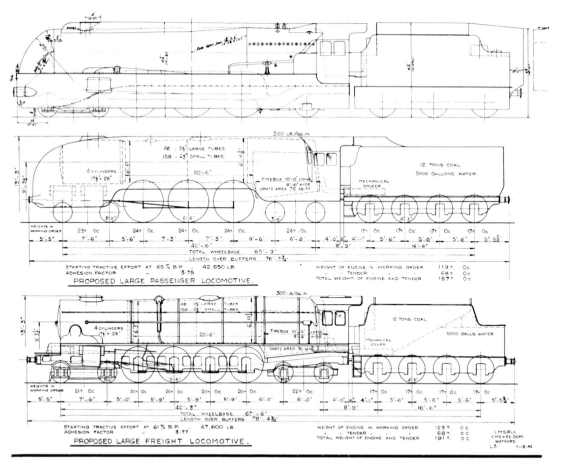

PROPOSED LARGE PASSENGER LOCOMOTIVE

300 LB/SQ.IN

48 - 5½" LARGE TUBES
158 - 2⅛" SMALL TUBES

4 CYLINDERS
17¼" × 28"

20'-6"

FIREBOX 10'-0" LONG
8'-6" WIDE
GRATE AREA 70 SQ.FT

MECHANICAL STOKER

12 TONS COAL
5000 GALLONS WATER.

STARTING TRACTIVE EFFORT AT 65% B.P. — 42,850 LB	WEIGHT OF ENGINE IN WORKING ORDER	119 T. 0c
ADHESION FACTOR — 3.75	TENDER	68 T. 0c
	TOTAL WEIGHT OF ENGINE AND TENDER	187 T. 0c

PROPOSED LARGE FREIGHT LOCOMOTIVE

300 LB/SQ.IN

48 - 5½" LARGE TUBES
158 - 2⅛" SMALL TUBES

4 CYLINDERS
17¾" × 28"

20'-6"

FIREBOX 10'-0" LONG
8'-6" WIDE

GRATE AREA 70 SQ.FT

MECHANICAL STOKER

12 TONS COAL

5000 GALLS WATER

STARTING TRACTIVE EFFORT AT 61% B.P. — 47,600 LB	WEIGHT OF ENGINE IN WORKING ORDER	123 T. 0c
ADHESION FACTOR — 3.77	TENDER	68 T. 0c
	TOTAL WEIGHT OF ENGINE AND TENDER	191 T. 0c

L.M.S.Ry.
C.M.E.& EE. DEPT
WATFORD
L.B. 11-12-42

Top: A drawing dating from 1935, and recently published in *The Power of the Duchesses* by David Jenkinson (Oxford Pub Co), depicts Stanier's initial thoughts on streamlining. The casing was evidently based upon contemporary German practice, with wheels and motion shrouded almost completely. The drawing was for a 1/24 scale model, and a portion, giving the side elevation is reproduced here. From the details of the original print it is apparent that this streamlining was proposed for 'Princess Royal' Pacifics Nos 6203-12, delivered from Crewe that year./*NRM*

Above: Drawing dated December 1942 and produced at the wartime headquarters at Watford, showing Stanier's thoughts on two of the types of new locomotive that might be required with the return of peace. Both stretched the LMSR loading gauge to the limits, and both required mechanical stokers, as it would have been beyond the strength of one man to fire them for any length of time. The 4-8-4 was visualised with bar frames and was apparently intended for fast container trains on the Anglo-Scottish run. The 4-6-4 was to be the high-speed and more powerful successor to the 'Princess Coronations'./*NRM*

Below: Stanier's practices were continued and improved by H.G. Ivatt in the final years of the LMSR, and many features were adopted for the BR Standard classes by R.A. Riddles, who had been Stanier's Principal Assistant before the war. 'Rebuilt Patriot' No 45527 *Southport* (minus nameplates) casts its shadow upon the cutting side as it approaches Shap summit with a freight; 1 September, 1964./*R. Sewell*

Above: Stanier left the LMSR before many Fowler 4-6-0 engines had received his improved boilers, but the fitting was continued by H. G. Ivatt, until all the 'Royal Scots' and 18 'Patriots' had received them (also two 'Jubilees'). 'Converted Royal Scot' class 4-6-0 No 46136 *The Border Regiment* darkens the sky as it passes Wreay with the Sunday Glasgow–Liverpool/Manchester express in October 1963./*P. J. Robinson*

Below: Stanier 'Black Fives' took part in the activities on Sunday, 11 August, 1968, when the last BR operated main line steam train was hauled by 'Black Fives' and by a BR 'Britannia' Pacific. Nos 44871 and 44781 were photographed approaching Ais Gill summit on the return journey from Carlisle. Thousands lined the sides of the tracks to witness this memorable day. A considerable number of 'Black Fives' have been privately preserved in working order by enthusiasts, and details of these, and other preserved Stanier engines can be found in Appendix 2./*D. Wharton*

4-6-2 Class 7P (BR Power Class 8P) Express Passenger Engines
Introduced: 1933
Total: 12
'Princess Royal'

Although the Fowler 'Royal Scot' class 4-6-0s were putting-up some good performances with trains of up to 420 tons on the Euston-Glasgow run it was nevertheless found to be desirable, by 1933, to have an engine of somewhat greater power, which would be capable of through working with trains of up to 500 tons, unaided. With the 'Royal Scots' the practice was to change engines at Carlisle because the fire, grate and ashpan of the 'Royal Scots' were likely to become over-choked with the products of 6½ to 7 hours continuous combustion. With a larger engine this would not be necessary and this offered potential savings in operating costs. For the new engine, the increased power was to be obtained by means of an improved boiler, with a large grate area, and this demanded a wide firebox. To accommodate this feature, and the added weight involved, a 4-6-2 wheel arrangement was decided upon, with a Bissel type trailing truck. One of the earliest specifications envisaged 6ft 9in diameter coupled wheels, but the eventual design was otherwise changed remarkably little. Clearly the design of the frames made use of

Below: The drawing depicts the series Nos 6203-11, when new. No 6212 was first delivered fitted with one of the two original boilers, rebuilt with dome and top feed.

work already done on the compound Pacific proposals of Hughes and Fowler, neither of which had materialised.

Authority for the construction of three Pacifics was granted in July 1932 and work went ahead with such purpose that no more than 17 months after William Stanier arrived on the LMSR, the first locomotive was completed at Crewe, to be followed later the same year by the second prototype. What was to have been the third identical engine was however earmarked for completion as an experimental turbine locomotive of comparable power (see Section 6).

As first constructed, the two prototypes, Nos 6200 *The Princess Royal* and 6201 *Princess Elizabeth,* clearly evidenced Stanier's Swindon background. There was a domeless taper boiler with low degree superheat, whilst a number of smaller features such as the axleboxes and bogie design, and the Swindon smokebox, were also introduced. But in certain other respects Stanier broke away from Swindon practices, for example by using four independent sets of Walschaerts long-travel valve gear and by retaining Derby type injectors. To reduce weight bar frames were used for the leading bogie.

A much improved cab design was introduced, with carefully arranged controls and tip-up seats

Heating surface, tubes
  Large and small: 2,167sq ft
  Firebox: 217sq ft
Total (evaporative): 2,384sq ft
Superheater: 623sq ft
  Superheater elements: 32
  Combined heating surfaces: 3,007sq ft
Grate area: 45sq ft
Tractive effort (at 85 per cent BP): 40,300lb

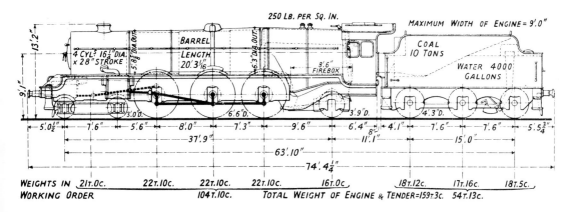

19

for both enginemen. Two side windows were provided, with a small folding window between them to act as a shield when the driver leant out beyond the cab side. Moreover, the taper boiler improved forward visibility. An interesting point about these engines is that alone of the large express power of the final years of the LMSR, they did not receive smoke deflectors at any stage in their careers.

Externally they had a decidedly handsome appearance, which was spoilt on the two prototypes by the initial version of the Stanier tender which lacked the high curved sides of the standard 4,000 gallons type later evolved. Once these had been replaced by the new high capacity Stanier design, with high sides curved in at the top to clear the loading gauge, they looked at their best. In their outline these engines had some similarity to the GWR 'King' class 4-6-0s, particularly at the leading end, but the massive rear end, with wide Belpaire firebox and additional external frame plates splayed outwards from the main frames, under the firebox and cab, gave a fine visual balance to the great length of the engine.

The engines were built as follows:

Nos 6200-1   Crewe   1933
Nos 6203-12   Crewe   1935

First of class withdrawn: 46204/10/1/2 (1961)
Last of class withdrawn: 46200 (1962)
Examples preserved: 46201/3

Left: 'Princess Royal' class Pacific No 6200 was the first Stanier locomotive to enter service, delivered to traffic from Crewe on 1 July, 1933. Portrayed here in works grey livery and prior to naming, is No 6200 as originally constructed, with low superheat domeless taper boiler. A dome-like casing housed the top feed clacks, and four 'pop' type safety valves were placed on the firebox. Features in common with the GWR 'King' class 4-6-0 included the diameter of the driving wheels, 6ft 6in, the four cylinders 16¼in diameter by 28in stroke, the working pressure of 250lb per sq in and the tractive effort of 40,300lb at 85 per cent working pressure./*LPC*

Below left: Whilst still carrying the original low superheat boiler, an experimental double exhaust system was tried out on No 6201. The exhaust of inside and outside cylinders was led separately into each half of the double chimney, instead of being combined at the base of the blastpipe in the more usual way. The experiment was not a success and the engine was quickly returned to normal. At one stage a streamlined outer casing was proposed to form a cowl around the chimney, on the smokebox top./*BR*

Above: No 6200 *The Princess Royal,* in original condition, hauling the up 'Royal Scot' express south of Rugby. The low-sided six wheel tender originally attached had roller bearings, and a coal capacity of 8 tons./*F.R. Hebron*

Below: The remaining 10 'Princess Royal' Pacifics were not delivered until 1935, and a number of important modifications were made to the design, following experience gained with the two prototypes. In particular the lesson had been learned that Swindon style low superheat did not suit LMSR operating conditions, and the number of elements was increased. The boiler was still domeless (steam was collected by means of a perforated pipe in the high front corner of the firebox; following GWR practice) and the barrel was shorter. The firebox heating surface was increased by creating a combustion chamber in the forward part of the firebox. Detail changes included the provision of new high sided tenders with a capacity of 9 tons of coal and 4,000 gallons of water; recessed pipes to the top feed clacks; larger brackets for the outside valve gear, and a redesigned reversing lever. No 6209 *Princess Beatrice* was photographed in the original condition of the second batch, heading north through the London suburbs./*E.R. Wethersett*

Above: Modifications in attempts to improve the steaming of the two prototypes included provision of a rebuilt boiler, 32 element superheater (off No 6200), with a steam dome and forward top feed housing, as seen here on No 6201 *Princess Elizabeth.* A new tender was fitted, with 9 tons coal capacity and 4,000 gallons water. The two original low sided tenders fitted to Nos 6200/1 were subsequently rebuilt with high curved sides and allocated to new Class 5 4-6-0s Nos. 5073/4 in 1935. The illustration shows the record breaking run of November 16, 1936, when the 401½ miles from Euston to Glasgow were covered in 5 hours 53 minutes, 38 seconds, with a seven coach load. (The man in the white coat on the footplate is R.A. Riddles, destined to be last CME of BR steam). No 6200 received the domeless boiler delivered for the experimental 'Turbomotive' (see section 6) at this time./*Ian Allan Library*

Below: No 6212 *Duchess of Kent* ran for some time with an experimental smoke-box door, secured by 10 lugs around the perimeter, instead of the central screw lock which was standard for Stanier engines. The illustration shows No 6212 pounding up the 1 in 200 to Castlemilk with the up 'Royal Scot'./*F.R. Hebron*

Right: At the end of 1936/early 1937 another change of tenders took place, when all 12 locomotives received new 10 ton, 4,000 gallon capacity tenders with higher curved sides. This gave a more powerful look to the ensemble as is well seen in this shot of No 46210 *Lady Patricia* climbing Shap with a Birmingham-Glasgow train, in early BR days, with LMSR black livery but carrying new number. No 6206 was the only member of the class fitted with a coal-pusher in the tender./*E. Treacy*

Below right: No 6205 *Princess Victoria* was the subject of another experiment, applied in 1938. The two inside sets of Walschaerts valve motion were replaced by rocking-levers, so that the outside valve motion operated the valves for the inside cylinders (a reversal of GWR practice, where the inside valve motion operated the valves for the outside cylinders). The modified motion bracket is clearly visible in this striking night scene, taken at Carlisle, as the locomotive (as BR No 46205, in green livery) awaits the 9.46pm Fish train, to work it forward to Crewe, 30 November, 1960./*C.P. Walker*

Above: Towards the end of January 1956, the Western Region experienced bogie troubles with their 'King' class 4-6-0s, and their temporary withdrawal for rectification resulted in a shortage of heavy express power. As a result, two 'Princess Royals', Nos 46207/10 were loaned to Old Oak Common for two months, and operated over both the West of England and the Birmingham main lines. Their duties included the 'Cornish Riviera' and No 46210 *Lady Patricia* was photographed passing Stoneycombe Quarries on Dainton Bank, with the down train, on 10 February, 1956./*D.S. Fish*

Top right: In BR days the class sported a variety of liveries, ranging from LNWR style lined black, to BR blue and then later, green. But during 1958 four of the class received crimson lake livery, and No 46207 *Princess Arthur of Connaught* was photographed in this beautiful livery, at Stafford. The engine is depicted in the final state of the

class, with steam dome and separate top feed on the boiler, and fitted with BR standard AWS equipment./*J.B. Bucknall*

Right: By early March, 1961, the entire class had been placed in store as a result of increased diesel availability. The summer traffic of the same year reprieved some of them temporarily, but scrapping commenced in the autumn. Much to everyone's surprise six locomotives were again returned to traffic at the end of January 1962, and were not finally withdrawn until the following autumn. No 46203 *Princess Margaret Rose,* in green livery, was one of the engines which enjoyed this unexpected Indian Summer, and was photographed leaving Carlisle with a down Euston–Perth train, in April 1962. No 46203 was unique in being the only LMSR Pacific to receive a heavy repair at Derby works, in the winter of 1951, when it received a new front to the frames./*S.C. Crook*

SECTION 2

2-6-0 Class 5F
Mixed-Traffic Engines
Introduced: 1933
Total: 40

Despite the fact that 245 mixed-traffic Moguls had been constructed to the successful Hughes/Fowler design of 1926—the well-known Horwich 'Crabs'—when a further 40 mixed-traffic locomotives were required in 1933, they were built to a new design, produced by the Horwich drawing office to Stanier's instructions.

The starting point in the design was to produce a locomotive of equivalent power to the Horwich 'Crabs' but with a boiler based upon Swindon practice, in principle if not in detail. The initial drawing was produced at Euston, outlining what the new Chief had in mind, and forwarded to Horwich for detail work to commence. This original drawing showed a domeless boiler with the safety valves housed in a domelike casing, and combined with the top feed clacks. Stanier was as yet an almost unknown personality at Horwich and, presumably in order to please him that office placed a typical GWR style 'coffeepot' safety valve casing upon the production drawings issued to Crewe, and engine No 13245 emerged from the erecting shops on 21 October, 1933 duly sporting this item of hardware. Far from being pleased, Stanier was very cross, and as soon as he saw it he ordered its removal and replacement by the dome-shaped casing which he had originally specified. He stressed that he had no desire to produce carbon copies of Swindon practice.

The first ten locomotives emerged with the safety valves on the boiler barrel with the modified casing; in the meantime Stanier had come to realise that there would not be room for this GWR type of safety valve on the larger locomotive boilers, in view of the LMSR loading gauge (particularly in Scotland) and he decided to adopt the short 'Pop' type of safety valves placed over the firebox, as was already standard practice on the LMSR, for all future construction.

The remaining 30 locomotives of the class appeared with the safety valves on the firebox and with top feed clacks covered by the casing that became standard for domeless boilers. It was one of these later locomotives, suitably renumbered for the occasion, that posed as No 13245 for the official photographs of the class. The 10 original boilers, with non-standard safety valves, were allowed to remain in service until they became due for their first major overhaul, as this was the earliest economic opportunity to modify them.

Outside Walschaerts long-travel valve gear was adopted, and the cylinders were arranged horizontally (the only Stanier design with this feature); they were 3in less in diameter than the cylinders on the 'Crabs', a reduction made possible by the higher working pressure of 225lb per sq in.

Heating surface, tubes
   Large and small: 1,216sq ft
   Firebox: 155sq ft
Total (evaporative): 1,371sq ft
Superheater: 224sq ft
   Superheater elements: 21
Combined heating surfaces: 1,595sq ft
Grate area: 27.8sq ft
Tractive effort (at 85 per cent BP): 26,288lb

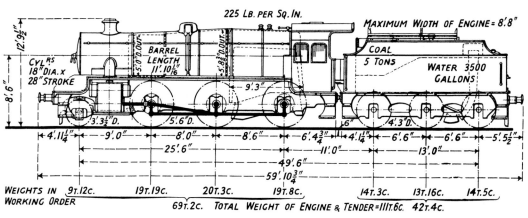

WEIGHTS IN WORKING ORDER: 9T.12C. / 19T.19C. / 20T.3C. / 19T.8C. / 14T.3C. / 13T.16C. / 14T.5C.
69T.2C. TOTAL WEIGHT OF ENGINE & TENDER = 111T.6C. 42T.4C.

The engines were built as follows:

Nos 13245-57	Crewe	1933
No 13260	Crewe	1933
No 13263	Crewe	1933
Nos 13258-59	Crewe	1934
Nos 13261-62	Crewe	1934
Nos 13264-84	Crewe	1934

When new, the power classification was 4F, subsequently altered to 5P4F (in 1934), then 5P5F

Below: The first Stanier Mogul as delivered from Crewe with a GWR-style safety valve bonnet. This was hastily removed after Stanier expressed his displeasure at such an obvious copy of Swindon tradition! For many years it was believed that all official photographs taken of the engine in this state had been destroyed./*NRM*

Bottom: One of the original batch of 10 locomotives, with the safety valves located on the boiler and combined with the top feed in a dome-like casing. This view of No 13248 working a Huddersfield–Manchester slow train was taken near Marsden. These engines were originally fitted with a crosshead vacuum pump on the left hand side, a feature removed from all Stanier engines, *circa* 1939, as it was found to be unnecessary./*P. Ransome-Wallis*

(in 1938/39) finally becoming 5F in late LMSR days. When new the class were allocated to all four operating divisions, as follows:

Nos 13245-13254	Northern Division
Nos 13255-13266	Midland Division
Nos 13267-13279	Western Division
Nos 13280-13284	Central Division

(Nos 13245-13254 at first had no water pick-up fitted.)

The Northern Division engines worked from Carlisle Kingmoor, their duties covering the old Caledonian main line, so that they were seen in Glasgow. Perth and Aberdeen.

Alone of Stanier's classes these engines were renumbered by the LMSR after construction, all others retaining their original numbers until nationalisation. Thus, in the 1934 renumbering scheme they became Nos 2945-2984.

Of all the Stanier classes they appear to have been the least recorded or photographed. Externally they were not particularly attractive machines—with their curiously low horizontal cylinders, shallow section running-plate and narrow Fowler tenders. The exterior of the cab resembled Horwich, rather than standard Stanier practice. Throughout their somewhat undistinguished lives they were in black livery. At first this was lined-out with red; in later LMSR days they were plain black. In BR days some received LNWR-style mixed-traffic lining-out. One interesting point is that this class had whistles fitted instead of the characteristic Caledonian bass siren used on all other Stanier engines.

Above: Also still sporting its original boiler, with safety valves combined with the top feed casing, No 2950 is shown in clean black livery, lined out in red./*P. Ransome-Wallis*

Top right: One of the second batch of 30 locomotives, with revised larger boiler design, having the safety valves relocated on top of the firebox. With modified boilers the engine plus tender weight was increased from 107.2 tons to 111.3 tons. No 42983 was photographed near Shap Wells with the down 7.40am Crewe–Carlisle class H through freight, on 26 May, 1952, with a 2-6-4T providing rear end assistance./*E.D. Bruton*

Centre right: In later years the class operated mainly in former LNWR areas, ranging from the North Wales coast to the Carlisle–London line and the West Midlands. No 42967 is seen somewhat further afield, at Chinley North Junction on the Saturdays only North Wales–Sheffield train, on 30 August, 1958./*N. Fields*

Bottom right: This rear three-quarters view of No 42962 emphasises the discrepancy in width of engine and tender. The tender was of Fowler pattern as used on the 'Crabs', whilst the cab sides were a Horwich feature, with their slight cutaway at the rear end. The engine was photographed whilst shunting at Chester General on 1 August, 1963./*S.D. Wainwright*

It is perhaps significant that no repeat orders were ever placed for this class, although no doubt the success of the 1934 'Black Fives' as mixed-traffic engines was one factor against them. A final point of interest is that late in their careers some examples of the class were overhauled at Swindon.

First of class withdrawn: 42976 (1963)
Last of class withdrawn: 42963 (1966)
Example preserved: 42968

SECTION 3

4-6-0 Class 5XP (BR Power Class 6P) Express Passenger Engines
Introduced: 1934
Total: 191*
'Jubilee'

The performance of the ex-LNWR 'Claughton' class was far from satisfactory and the type was unecomic in maintenance; although some were improved by fitting larger boilers or by fitting Caprotti valve gear in place of Walschaerts. Derby took the opportunity that presented itself in 1929, when it was agreed that two 'Claughtons' should have new frames, and they fitted these with the bigger boiler in conjunction with frames of the type for Fowler's 'Royal Scot' class, thereby producing an improved version of the 'Claughton', soon to become known as the 'Baby Scot', and later officially known as the 'Patriot' class. A number of components from the two displaced 'Claughtons' were retained in the rebuilding, which proved to be very successful. At the very first meeting of the LMS Locomotive Committee that Stanier attended, in January 1932, the conversion of a further 15 was approved. The 1933 programme had a further 25 included and then in May 1933 it was decided to build 15 more, instead of 10 4-6-0s (see Section 4) and five 2-8-0s (see Section 7). Stanier introduced a number of changes in the design, in particular for the axleboxes, wheels and bogies. Nos 5502-11 did not have the improved bogie, as they were too advanced in construction.

*Later reduced to 189 when 2 locomotives were rebuilt to Class 6P. (See Section 12).

Meanwhile, design work was put in hand for a Stanier version of the class, known at first as 'Improved Claughtons', and this was completed in time for the last five 'Patriots' on order to be built with taper-boilers, using the existing frame design. Thus, in accordance with his own principles a low-degree superheat domeless taper boiler replaced the Fowler parallel boilers and various smaller items were redesigned, such as the cab and tender. But basically the new Stanier 3-cylinder 5XP was a direct development of the Fowler engines.

In volume one of his book *Locomotive Panorama*, E. S. Cox has lucidly described how the initial disappointing results of this design proved to be the chief factor which caused Stanier to rethink the merits of Swindon-style low-degree superheat. As first introduced, the Stanier engines proved inferior to the 'Baby Scots' so far as steam production was concerned. Several factors were involved. A reduction of nearly 100°F in steam temperature, due to employment of a superheater of only 14-elements (compared to 24-elements on the 'Baby Scots'), resulted in a pure loss of thermal efficiency; whilst the taper boiler design produced a reduction in the total tube-free area

Heating surface, tubes
  Large and small: 1,279sq ft
  Firebox: 181sq ft
Total (evaporative): 1,460sq ft
Superheater: 300sq ft
  Superheater elements: 24
Combined heating surfaces: 1,760sq ft
Grate area: 31.0sq ft
Tractive effort (at 85 per cent BP): 26,610lb
(*Note*: Typical dimensions for class, after fitting with domed boilers)

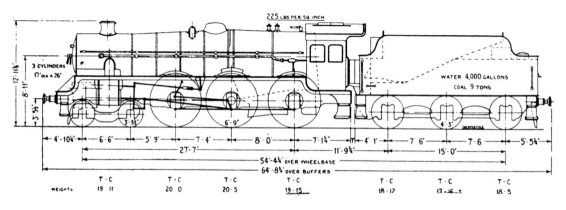

30

Above: The first of the class No 5552 (un-named), in original condition with low-degree superheat domeless taper boiler; at the head of a container train. The locomotive has its original narrow 3,500 gallon Fowler tender attached, which it retained until 1958. No 5552 ran as such for some 4 months, then exchanged identities with No 5642./*Ian Allan Library*

Below: The second No 5552 was built as No 5642 and then exchanged identities with the original engine. Named *Silver Jubilee,* in honour of the Silver Jubilee of King George V, it was finished in a special livery of glossy black embellished with chromium fittings, including the top-feed cover, the steam pipes, boiler bands, hand-rails and relief numerals and lettering. No 5552 *Silver Jubilee* is seen here on shed at Camden in this unique finish./*P. Ransome-Wallis*

through which the hot gases passed from firebox to smokebox. Finally, there were draughting troubles because the blastpipe and chimney dimensions were based upon the Swindon formula for four-beat engines and did not suit the six-beats of the 3-cylinder design.

Stanier did not immediately realise that these were the basic causes of the troubles, and a series of hit-and-miss modifications and trials was proceeded with in attempts to discover why the new class did not perform as expected. Meanwhile the engines had been ordered in some quantity, and a large number were delivered to the original specification whilst experiments were continued to resolve the problem. No testing facilities then existed comparable to the mobile and stationary testing-plants of the later days of steam; it was largely a case of trial and error. After various attempts (some of which only worsened matters), a successful combination of improved boiler design (with 24-element superheater), and reduced blast-pipe diameter, transformed the 'Jubilees' into competent locomotives which performed their role of intermediate express power efficiently for the rest of their careers.

As first built the engines had domeless taper boilers with a tube heating surface of 1,462.5sq ft, a firebox heating surface of 162.4sq ft and a 14-element superheater with a heating surface of 227sq ft (except Nos 5642-46 which had 21-element superheaters; figures being 1,372, 162 and 256sq ft respectively). The grate area was 29.5sq ft. The working pressure was 225lb per sq in, and the tractive effort at 85 per cent boiler pressure was 26,610lb. As modified, after a series of attempts with various combinations of 2- and 3-row superheaters; different tube proportions and different blastpipe sizes, the final boilers had the dimensions listed at the end of this section. The blastpipe diameter was reduced to 7⅞in as part of the attempts to improve the steaming.

One boiler, first used on No 5677, had 28-elements, a distinction it retained throughout its life; being fitted to several different locomotives in the course of time. The 108 14-element boilers were all reconstructed with 24-element superheaters and with domes but the five 21-element boilers were not altered, although they could of course be exchanged amongst engines Nos 5552-5664, and did so. To create spare domeless boilers for these engines, nine locomotives Nos 5567/90, 5607/8/16/21/22/39/40/57 were modified to take the sloping throatplate type (see page 10) in 1936-7, (Nos 5607/12/22 subsequently reverted to vertical throatplate boilers), whilst No 5610 was a later conversion in 1943.

Below: In charge of a return excursion to Leicester, No 5652 (un-named) is seen at Bushey on 10 August, 1936. The engine is in original condition with domeless boiler, and with Stanier tender. Nameplates were attached to locomotives of the early batches after they had entered service./*E. R. Wethersett*

Right: From No 5665 onwards, the 'Jubilees' were built with improved boilers with dome and separate top feed. No 5684 *Jutland* was fitted with an experimental Kylchap double blastpipe and chimney for a while, in 1937. In conjunction with incorrect tube proportions, a very real disadvantage over the orthodox single chimney was disclosed, in the form of excessive spark-throwing and build-up of ash in the smokebox. This double chimney arrangement was therefore quickly abandoned./*BR*

Below right: No 5664 *Nelson* was the last of the engines to be delivered with a domeless taper boiler, in 1935. By 1937, when this photograph was taken, it had received a modified boiler with separate dome and top feed. Illustrated leaving Elstree Tunnel with the 2.30pm St Pancras–Kettering on 5 June, 1937./*E.R. Wethersett*

All three 17in by 26in cylinders had separate sets of Walschaerts long-travel valve gear. The drive was divided; the inside cylinder was located well forward and drove the front single-throw crank axle, and the two outside cylinders drove onto the crank-pins in the centre pair of coupled wheels.

No less than four different tender designs were attached to this class. These were 4,000 gallon and 3,500 gallon (short wheelbase) versions of the Stanier tender, and the 3,500 gallon Fowler tender; also a high flat-sided version of the Fowler tender, which eliminated the coal-rails. The Fowler tenders were off the 'Royal Scot' class (except the high-sided variety and those of Nos 5552-56 which were built new for these engines) and were exchanged to provide the 'Scots' with 4,000 gallon Stanier tenders.

The 'Jubilees' operated on all four divisions of the LMSR, although somewhat more route-restricted than the versatile 'Black Fives'.

The engines were built as follows:

Nos 5552-5556	Crewe	1934
Nos 5557-5593	North British	1934
Nos 5594-5606	North British	1935
Nos 5607-5646	Crewe	1934
Nos 5647-5654	Crewe	1935
Nos 5655-5664	Derby	1935
Nos 5665-5681	Crewe	1935
Nos 5682-5742	Crewe	1936

Nos 5552-5664 were delivered with domeless boilers. Nos 5665-5742 were built new with improved boilers, with separate dome and top feed.

First of class withdrawn: 45637 (1952)
Last of class withdrawn: 45562 (1967)
Examples preserved: 45593/6 45690/9

Below: Fitted with the high-sided version of the narrow Fowler tender, No 5609 *Gilbert and Ellice Islands* was photographed leaving Bristol Temple Meads on the northbound 'Devonian', in prewar days./*G.H. Soole*

Right: A freak combination of boiler mountings. No 5578 *United Province* with domed boiler, but with the original style of dome-shaped top feed casing placed forward of the steam dome proper; giving a double-domed effect. /*P. Ransome-Wallis*

Below right: The LMSR Mobile Testing Plant provided much valuable data on steam locomotive performance in postwar days. No 5667 *Jellicoe* is shown attached to the train with the special corridor tender, and with wind gauges mounted ahead of the smokebox. The engine is in postwar LMSR black livery but the tender retains the original crimson lake./*BR*

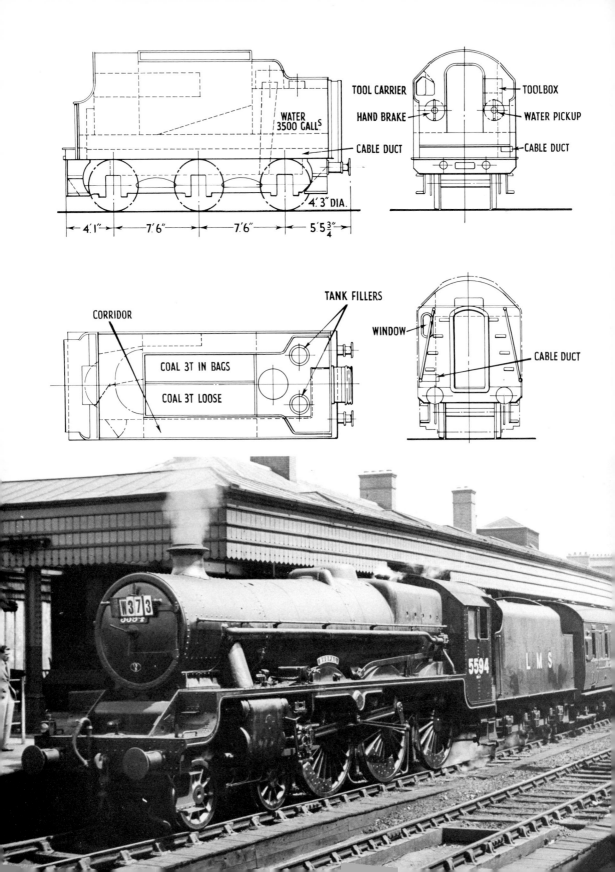

WATER 3500 GALLS

CABLE DUCT

4' 3" DIA.

4' 1"   7' 6"   7' 6"   5' 5¾"

TOOL CARRIER

HAND BRAKE

TOOLBOX

WATER PICKUP

CABLE DUCT

CABLE DUCT

CORRIDOR

TANK FILLERS

COAL 3T IN BAGS

COAL 3T LOOSE

WINDOW

CABLE DUCT

N373

5594

LMS

Left: Stanier's unique corridor tender, produced for locomotive testing purposes, and still utilised as such in early BR days./*BR*

Below left: 'Jubilee' class 4-6-0 No 5594 *Bhopal* had the distinction of being the only LMSR locomotive to receive crimson lake livery after the war. It was finished in an experimental style, with sans-serif lettering and numerals and was fully lined-out on one side only. At the same time another 'Jubilee', No 5573 *Newfoundland,* was finished in an experimental blue-grey lined in maroon and gilt. No 5594 (showing the plain crimson side) was photographed at the head of a South Wales–Manchester Saturday special, about to depart from Shrewsbury on 5 July 1947./*J.H. Platts*

Above: Until an easing of route-restrictions allowed 'Converted Scots', and 'Britannias' to operate over the Midland main-line, the 'Jubilees' formed the mainstay of express power, ably assisted by the 'Black Fives'. No 45694 *Bellerophon* makes a splendid picture as it leaves St Pancras with the 4.50pm down Bradford restaurant car express, on 25 August 1948. As part of experiments to determine new liveries for the nationalised railways, the engine was painted bright apple green with LNWR-style lining, and the carriages were in chocolate and cream./*E.D. Bruton*

Below: No 45719 *Glorious* is seen passing Bessy Ghill, near Thrimby Grange on the northern climb to Shap, with the 11.10am Edinburgh Princes St–Liverpool Exchange express. The engine is paired with one of the narrow high-sided Fowler 3,500 gallon tenders./*J.E. Wilkinson*

Above: In 1958 it was decided that a change of tenders should take place, for London Midland Region 'Jubilees'. These received 4,000 gallon Stanier tenders taken from 8F 2-8-0s which then took the 3,500 gallon Fowler tenders that some had previously run with. No 45616 *Malta G.C.* still had a small Fowler tender when this photograph was taken as the engine left Leicester London Road with a northbound express, on 21 April, 1956./*P.H. Groom*

Below: Chimney oddity on No 45561 *Saskatchewan;* photographed at York. The usual Stanier pattern has been replaced by a standard BR casting. An expedient that became necessary once the originals wore out./*E. Treacy*

Bottom: In addition to No 5684, already mentioned, at least four other 'Jubilees' carried double blastpipes and chimneys at various times. Nos 5553, 45596, 45722 (only on trials), and 5742. No 45596 *Bahamas* was out-shopped from Crewe in 1961, fitted with a double blastpipe and chimney, and is seen here working a down Blackpool express past Carpenders Park, on 15 August, 1964./*P.J. Russell*

SECTION 4

4-6-0 Class 5
Mixed-Traffic Engines
Introduced: 1934
Total: 842
'Black Fives'

The need for a 'maid-of-all-work' mixed-traffic locomotive was high on the list of priorities but despite several proposals put forward since 1923 an acceptable design had not materialised. Beames' Caprotti rebuilding of the ex-LNWR 'Prince of Wales' class came near to acceptance but it never really had the makings of a good engine. Although 10 were initially included in the 1933 building programme, Derby produced designs for an alternative version; in the event the order was held over and some more 5XP 'Patriots' were built instead.

Stanier soon had a design drawn up capable of operating over virtually the whole system, on a wide variety of duties ranging from express passenger to branch line freight and stopping trains, which would replace numerous pre-Grouping engines of widely different types. The finalised design, with very straightforward 2-cylinder layout, and incorporating the taper boiler and other features introduced to the LMSR by Stanier, proved to be one of the most successful and popular classes of locomotive ever constructed. Contrary to popular belief, this was not the largest class of Stanier designed locomotives, being exceeded by 10 examples by the 8F 2-8-0s, of which—all told—852 were built. Also considered was a lighter 4-6-0 for Scotland to replace various Caledonian and Highland 4-6-0

classes, and 10 were authorised but soon deferred. The design became unnecessary when it was decided to rebuild a number of bridges which allowed an extended route availability for the heavier engine.

In common with early examples of his other designs of the 1933-35 period, the first Class 5s (or to use their now familiar nickname, 'Black Fives'), had domeless low-degree superheat taper boilers and smokebox regulators. Unlike the 5XP 'Jubilees', however, the steaming of even the initial low-degree superheat examples was excellent. But Stanier soon realised that what had proved adequate in power output and efficiency for Swindon locomotives, burning good Welsh coal, did not suffice under LMSR operating conditions.

As first built, there was a total evaporative heating surface of 1,616sq ft, comprising a tube heating surface of 1,460sq ft and a firebox heating surface of 156sq ft. The 14-element superheater heating surface was 228sq ft, and the grate area was 27.8sq ft. Working pressure was 225lb and the tractive effort at 85 per cent working pressure was 25,455lb. Two outside cylinders, 18½in diameter by 28in stroke with Walschaerts long-travel valve gear, were provided.

Heating surface, tubes
  Large and small: 1,478.7sq ft
  Firebox: 171.3sq ft
Total (evaporative): 1,650.0sq ft
Superheater: 359.3sq ft
Superheater elements: 28
Combined heating surfaces: 2,009.3sq ft
Grate area: 28.65sq ft
Tractive effort (at 85 per cent BP): 25,455lb
(*Note*: Typical dimensions for engines fitted with domed boilers.)

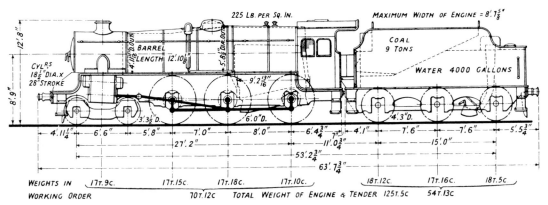

Experience soon revealed the need to modify the design, as mentioned above, and several boiler designs were tried. Finally, the superheater surface was increased to 348sq ft, with 28 elements; the tube heating surface was increased to 1,479sq ft; the firebox heating surface was increased to 171sq ft and the total evaporative heating surface became 1,650sq ft. The grate area was increased to 28.7sq ft. These were the main changes made, but other variations existed with individual members of this extremely large class. As in the case of the 'Jubilees' a number of the earlier engines were modified to create a pool of spare domeless boilers, and a surprising number of the class ran their entire lives with domeless boilers.

Construction proceeded steadily, and the class became a familiar sight practically everywhere on the LMSR system. With their moderate size, weight and length, the term ubiquitous has frequently been used to describe the 'Black Fives', with complete justification. After Stanier had finally retired from LMSR affairs in 1944, C. E. Fairburn continued with their construction, unchanged. When H. G. Ivatt succeeded Fairburn he introduced some modifications and also a number of experimental versions. But the basic design remained as Stanier had conceived it, and construction continued into the early years of the BR era.

Above: The first batch of 'Black Fives' to actually enter service were Nos 5020-5069, built by Vulcan Foundry. These had low-degree superheat domeless taper boilers, and at first they had the pipes to the top feed clacks outside the boiler-cladding. The chimney was slightly taller than on later engines of the class./*Ian Allan Library*

Below: Another example of the first batch of 'Black Fives', delivered from Vulcan Foundry. No 5042 seen working a Midland line express at Elstree, still in original condition with tall chimney, etc./*E.R. Wethersett*

Right: The later domeless engines had a smaller chimney, and the pipes to the top feed clacks were recessed into the boiler cladding. No 45211 was photographed passing Black Rock with a Manchester–Leeds semi-fast./*K. Field*

Below right: From No 5225 onwards, all 'Black Fives' were built new with improved boilers; with separate dome and top feed. No 5232 was photographed at Oxenholme in prewar days, with a down passenger train. The tenders for the class were of standard Stanier pattern, with curved high sides, although early drawings showed a Fowler tender. The capacity was 4,000 gallons and 9 tons. First livery of the class was black, with red lining, and it was this that gave them the nicknames 'Black Staniers' or 'Black Fives', to distinguish them from the crimson lake 5XPs./*F.R. Hebron*

The engines were built as follows:

Nos 5000-5019	Crewe	1935
Nos 5020-5069	Vulcan Foundry	1934/5
Nos 5070-5074	Crewe	1935
Nos 5075-5124	Vulcan Foundry	1935
Nos 5125-5224	Armstrong Whitworth	1935

All these, Nos 5000-5224 inclusive, were built with domeless boilers. All the locomotives listed below were built new with domed boilers and separate top feed.

Nos 5225-5451	Armstrong Whitworth	1936-38
Nos 5452-5471	Crewe	1938
Nos 5472-5491	Derby	1943
Nos 5492-5499	Derby	1944
Nos 4800-4825	Derby	1944
Nos 4826-4835	Crewe	1944
Nos 4836-4860	Crewe	1944
Nos 4861-4920	Crewe	1945
Nos 4921-4931	Crewe	1946
Nos 4932-4943	Horwich	1945
Nos 4944-4962	Horwich	1946
Nos 4963-4981	Crewe	1946
Nos 4982-4990	Horwich	1946
Nos 4991-4999	Horwich	1947

The locomotives built from late 1946 onwards incorporated certain refinements, such as self-cleaning smokeboxes, rocking grates and self-emptying ashpans. The following batches incorporated these modifications and included a number of experimental versions by H. G. Ivatt. Certain engines were fitted with electrical lighting.

Nos 4768-4782	Crewe	1947
Nos 4783-4799	Horwich	1947
Nos 4758-4766	Crewe	1947

Fitted with Timken roller bearings. Nos 4765/6 had double blastpipe and chimney.

No 4767	Crewe	1947

Outside Stephenson link motion; double blast-pipe and chimney; Timken roller bearings.

Nos M4748-M4753 and Nos 44754-44757	Crewe	1948

Caprotti poppet-valve gear. Timken roller bearings. Nos 44755-44757 had double chimneys.

Nos 44738-44747	Crewe	1948

Caprotti poppet-valve gear. Plain bearings.

Nos 44728-44737	Crewe	1949
Nos 44718-44727	Crewe	1949
Nos 44698-44717	Horwich	1948/9
Nos 44688-44697	Horwich	1950

Timken roller bearings on the driving axles only.

Nos 44686-44687	Horwich	1951

Below: This domeless example No 5005 has the later type of top feed casing instead of the more usual dome-shaped version./*P. Ransome-Wallis*

Top right: Boilers were swapped around frequently when an engine went into works for heavy repair. An example is this Ivatt-version boiler (with top feed moved nearer the chimney) carried by an earlier Stanier-built locomotive. No 45469 was double-heading with No 44702 on an Edinburgh–Greenock Special, when it was photographed at Currie on 9 May, 1964./*D. Cross*

Below right: A broadside view of 'Black Five' No 44874 (double-heading with No 45017) as it climbs towards Standedge Tunnel, near Clayton Bride, with an SLS railtour from Birmingham on 4 August 1968./*M. Shackleton*

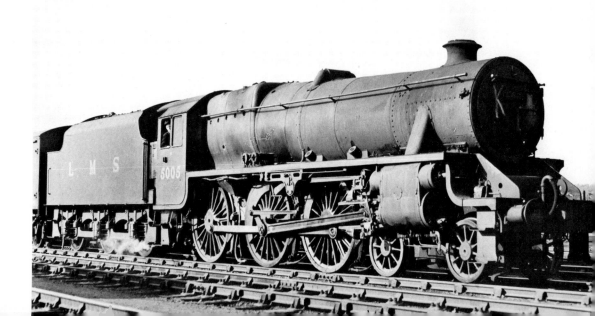

Caprotti poppet-valve gear; Skefko bearings; double blastpipe and chimney. (Last of class constructed).

Nos 44678-44685   Horwich   1950
Skefko roller bearings.

Left: An unusual angle to view a Class 5, which emphasises the clean lines of the design. No splashers were necessary as (except on the Caprotti engines), the running-plate cleared the 6ft driving wheels. No 44946 was photographed at Patricroft./*J.R. Carter*

Below left: Four of the class were named in LMSR days (a fifth was widely rumoured to have carried the name *Queen's Edinburgh,* but this was never satisfactorily confirmed). This superb night scene shows No 45156 *The Ayrshire Yeomanry,* still with domeless boiler, standing in Patricroft shed yard before leaving for the last time, when Patricroft was closed down on 29 May, 1968./*J.R. Carter*

Below: 'Black Five' No 45253 took part in the 1948 Locomotive Exchanges; with highly-satisfactory results between Bristol and Plymouth, yet giving an uncharacteristically poor performance on the Great Central line! It is seen here leaving Parson's Tunnel, Dawlish, with a Bristol–Plymouth express, whilst operating on the Western Region./*E. Oldham*

Nos 44668-44677   Horwich   1950
Skefko roller bearings on driving axles only.
Nos 44658-44667   Crewe   1949

To accommodate the Timken cannon-type axleboxes under the ashpan, used on some locomotives, the trailing driving wheels on these final batches were moved 4in back. On the Caprotti engines the boiler was raised 2in higher.

As already mentioned, the 'Black Fives' were to be found virtually all over the system, and they were also favourite motive power for through workings with excursion trains to 'foreign' destinations such as the South Coast resorts. In certain places turntables had to be lengthened before they could be accommodated.

First of class withdrawn: 45401 (1961)
Last of class withdrawn: 44781, 44871, 45110 (1968)
Examples preserved: 44767, 44806, 44871, 44932, 45000, 45025, 45110, 45212, 45231, 45305, 45379, 45407, 45428.

Above: Temporary withdrawal of the 'Merchant Navy' class Pacifics on the Southern Region, following discovery of a serious defect, resulted in the loan of seven 'Black Fives' to the SR in 1953, together with other classes. No 45051 was photographed at Brookwood with the second portion of the 3pm down West of England express from Waterloo on 23 May, 1953./*R. W. Beaton*

Below: As already mentioned the class gained its nickname from the black livery carried. In fact only three examples were ever painted any other colour whilst in BR ownership. These were selected to display proposals for a new BR livery, in 1948. No M4762 was finished in Southern Railway malachite green; No M4763 was in LNER apple green, and No M4764 was in GWR brunswick green. They

were fully lined-out on one side only, and displayed at Kensington Addison Road; afterwards going into normal traffic. No M4763 is illustrated, working the 7.45pm Llandudno–Chester stopping train, near Maes Du, on 8 June, 1948./*E.D. Bruton*

Above right : No 44986, paired with a self-weighing tender, photographed at Chester working a Class H through goods train on 1 June, 1962./*J.R. Carter*

Right: No 4767, built during H.G. Ivatt's period of office, was an experimental engine, with outside Stephensons link motion, Timken roller bearings, electric lighting and double chimney and blastpipe./*E.S. Cox Collection*

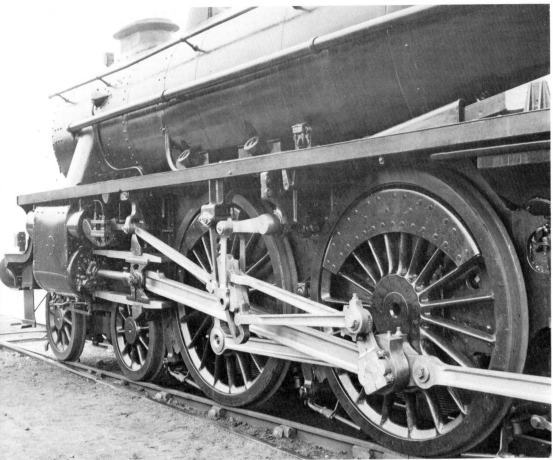

Above: 'Black Five' No 44766 at Bangor on 6 August 1952 with a Bank Holiday excursion from Manchester. One of two engines with double chimney and Timken roller bearings. Note the electric lighting and headcode discs./*E. Treacy*

Top right: Many 'Black Fives' survived their entire career with domeless boilers, but with improved heating surfaces. No 45190 is illustrated, in BR lined black livery./*J.B. Bucknall*

Right: H.G. Ivatt's modifications did not always improve the appearance of Stanier's design, nevertheless No 44749 makes a pleasing picture in clean lined black livery at Dillicar near Tebay, with a Carlisle–Crewe parcels train; 9 September, 1959. One of a batch delivered in 1948 from Crewe with Caprotti poppet-valve gear and Timken roller bearings./*J.E. Wilkinson*

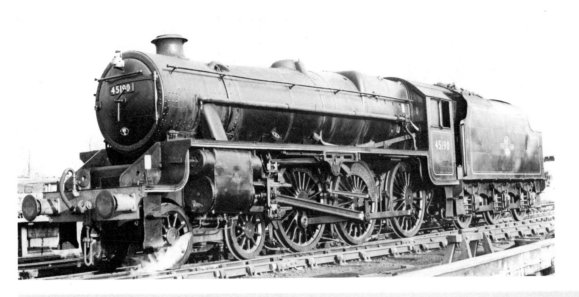

Above: In addition to Caprotti poppet-valve gear and Timken roller bearings, three locomotives, Nos 44755-57, were built with double blastpipes and chimneys and electric lighting. No 44756 was photographed passing Bingley, Yorks., with the down 'Thames–Clyde Express'./*W. Hubert Foster*

Below: Final 'Black Five' variant by H.G. Ivatt, with Caprotti poppet-valve gear. Skefko bearings and double chimney; built at Horwich, 1951. The raised running boards drastically altered the appearance of the engine, and foreshadowed the design of the later BR Standard classes. No 44687 was photographed at Birmingham New Street, at the head of the 'Pines Express' in June 1951./*A.W. Flowers*

2-6-4T Class 4P
Passenger Tank Engines
Introduced: 1934
Total: 37

The 1933 locomotive building programme included a batch of Fowler 2-cylinder 2-6-4Ts, and Stanier used this authorisation to produce instead five new 3-cylinder taper boilered 2-6-4Ts. The 1934 programme authorised a further 32 of similar type. Although it is believed that Stanier had the specific and urgent need for new power for the Southend line foremost in his mind, the first five engines were not allocated there immediately. The batch of 32 was however specifically ordered for that purpose.

These massive tank engines had a 3-cylinder arrangement which, it was believed, would provide high acceleration. Subsequent experience proved that the earlier Fowler design of 2-6-4T, which had a straightforward 2-cylinder layout, was capable of equal performance, and later Stanier 2-6-4Ts were of 2-cylinder type (see Section 8). Nevertheless the 3-cylinder series were well liked by their crews and they were the mainstay of the Southend line services for many years.

The design in general followed the new practice initiated under Stanier's direction; with a domeless low-degree superheat boiler and Walschaerts long-travel valve gear. As built, the boilers had a heating surface of 1,137sq ft, comprising a tube heating surface of 1,000sq ft and firebox heating surface of 137sq ft. The superheater heating surface was 153.5sq ft. The grate area was 25sq ft. Tractive effort at 85 per cent of the boiler pressure was 24,600lbs. Modifications to the boiler later raised the total heating surface to 1,265sq ft, (see principal dimensions; below). Drawings issued in late LMSR days showed the class fitted with domed boilers, but only three were altered, Nos 2505/13/23, in order to provide spare domeless boilers, the others remaining domeless for their entire working lives.

The three 16in by 26in cylinders all drove the centre coupled axle; the two outside cylinders had two-bar crossheads but the inside cylinders had a single-bar arrangement.

As mentioned earlier, although the class will always be associated with the Southend line, they did in fact wander much farther afield from time to time. When new, the first five locos were allocated to Watford for suburban duties out of Euston and Broad Street and were also used for a time on St Pancras suburban duties, and during World War 2 at a time when traffic on the Southend line was more restricted, there were

---

Heating surface, tubes
  Large and small: 1,126.0sq ft
  Firebox: 139.0sq ft
Total (evaporative): 1,265.0sq ft
Superheater: 185.0sq ft
  Superheater elements: 18
Combined heating surfaces: 1,450.0sq ft
Grate area: 26.7sq ft
Tractive effort (at 85 per cent BP): 24,600lb

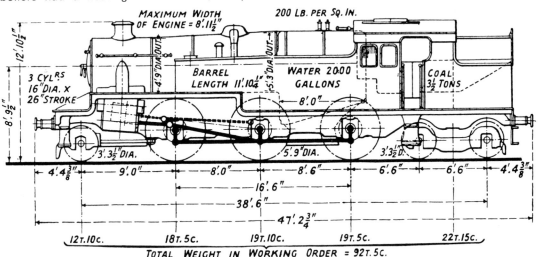

examples allocated to Kentish Town, Cricklewood, Derby, Nottingham, Kirkby, Manningham and Saltley. In 1951 two examples were transferred on loan to the Scottish Region in exchange for two Fairburn 2-6-4Ts; Nos 42530/5 were allocated to Greenock (Ladyburn). No water pick-up gear was fitted to these engines.

The entire class was built at Derby in 1934.

First of class withdrawn: 42512 (1960)
Last of class withdrawn: 42536 (1962)
Example preserved: 42500

Top left: The first 10 locomotives had straight sides to the bunker tops, a feature clearly discernible in this view of No 2502. Another early feature was the location of the pipes to the top feed clacks, outside the boiler cladding./*P. Ransome-Wallis*

Left: Nos 2500-2524 were constructed with full-length cab doors, similar to the final batch of the Fowler 2-6-4Ts. Complaints of excessive heat resulted from this, and the final batch of 12 had modified cabs. No 2524 was photographed at Plaistow on 6 April 1935, with characteristic LTSR line destination board above the buffer beam./*E.R. Wethersett*

Above: Working bunker-to-bunker two Stanier 3-cylinder tanks head for Southend via Tilbury. The leading engine is No 2527, one of the final batch of 12 locomotives with revised cab design, with a cutaway section in the rear cab side sheets, and waist-high doors./*E.R. Wethersett*

Centre right: To improve vision when running bunker first the sides of the bunker tops were cranked inwards on all engines from No 2510 onwards (and on the later 2-cylinder version). This feature is clearly shown in this picture of No 42512 working bunker first on a Fenchurch Street–Tilbury train, passing Campbell Road Junction, 21 July, 1951. The four leading carriages are ex-LTSR stock./*P.T. Lynch*

Bottom right: Final days of steam on the Southend line. Under 25 kv catenary. No 42519 in BR lined-black livery is seen ascending Laindon bank, at Dunton, on 4 March, 1961, at the head of the down 2.25pm slow. Note that the angled airvent pipes have been removed from the top of the side-tanks./*P.J. Paton*

SECTION 6

4-6-2 Class 7P
Express Passenger Engine
Introduced: 1935
Total: 1
'Turbomotive'

Stanier's sole venture into the field of unconventional motive power, the 'Turbomotive' (as it became popularly known), was all the more remarkable for having one of the longest and most successful careers of any experimental locomotive produced this century.

It was the success of a non-condensing turbine locomotive of the Ljungstrom type, on the Swedish Grangesburg—Öxelösund Railway, in 1932, which prompted the LMSR experiment. Stanier visited Sweden to see the engine at work, together with a representative of the Metropolitan-Vickers Company, which also had an interest in the progress being made in Sweden.

As already mentioned on page 19, the LMSR had originally planned to construct three prototype 'Princess Royal' class Pacifics at Crewe in 1933. But following the favourable impression made by the Swedish turbine locomotive, the decision was taken to cancel the third orthodox engine, and to produce instead a non-condensing turbine engine.

The boiler, wheels, frames and numerous mechanical parts were basically similar to the 'Princess Royal'' class, but in other respects the 'Turbomotive' was radically different. The contract for the turbine equipment was placed with Metropolitan Vickers, and the locomotive was completed at Crewe in June 1935, at a cost of £20,383, compared to £8,538 each for the second batch of 'Princess Royals', Nos 6203-6212. Although the 'Turbomotive' was allocated No 6202 in the 'Princess Royal' class, it was never officially named.

The principle of turbine drive was one which allowed an even torque on the driving axle, thereby eliminating the hammer-blow which was a usual characteristic of conventional cylinders and reciprocating valve motion. (Actually some reciprocating locomotives had nil hammer-blow). Thus a greater proportion of the total weight of the engine was available for adhesion. An axle load of 24 tons (later reduced to 23.3 tons) was permitted, compared with a maximum of 22½ tons for conventional steam, and roller bearings were fitted throughout to engine and tender. The tender was of standard Stanier design.

As no condenser was fitted there was a reduced theoretical thermal efficiency, but this

Below: The diagram shows the second boiler, with dome and 40-element superheater.

Right: Prior to entering service the 'Turbomotive' showed her paces before the press cameras, on 28 June 1935, at Camden. As first built the engine had a domeless boiler of similar dimensions to those fitted to the second batch of 'Princess Royal' 4-6-2s, Nos 6203-12, with a 32-element superheater./*Author's collection*

Heating surface, tubes
   Large and small: 1,951sq ft
   Firebox: 217sq ft
Total (evaporative): 2,168sq ft
Superheater: 577sq ft
   Superheater elements: 40
Combined heating surfaces: 2,745sq ft
Grate area: 45sq ft

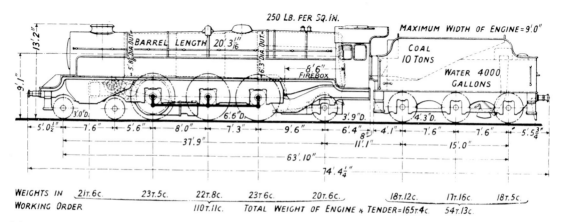

allowed a considerable simplification in design. There were two turbines, at the front of the engine. The main turbine, for forward running, was located on the left-hand side and had a shaft horsepower of 2,000 when using steam at 250lb pressure and with a temperature of 750deg F. A treble reduction gear of the double helical type, permanently in mesh, transmitted to the torque to the leading coupled driving wheel. The reverse turbine was located on the right-hand side, and was much smaller. The reverse turbine was normally idle and could only be brought into use when the engine was stationary, by means of a dog clutch. When the reverse turbine was in action the steam supply to the forward turbine was cut off, and the blades idled in the opposite direction. Steam entered the turbine by means of six valves, capable of being opened or closed one-by-one from the driver's controls in the cab. The number of valves open was varied to suit the power demand.

All the transmission shafts and gears were enclosed in a suspended case and lubricated by means of a closed force-feed oiling circuit, activated by three pumps, two of which were steam driven and worked continuously, even when the locomotive was stationary. Steam for train heating was bled-off the turbine exhaust. As no condenser was employed, the turbine exhaust was turned-up through the chimney, and provided draught for the fire. But because of the low pressure of the turbine exhaust an automatically variable double blastpipe and double chimney was found to be necessary.

Externally the 'Turbomotive' was one of the neatest modern steam locomotives, although it would be true to say that it had a definite 'best side'—the left-hand side, with the long casing housing the forward turbine. In his book *The Locomotive* (Studio, 1937) the American industrial designer Raymond Loewy was lavish indeed with his praise, describing it as '. . . one of the most beautiful pieces of machinery ever de-

Below: This shot of the 'Turbomotive' shows the second boiler, with steam dome and separate top feed, and the long casing housing the large forward turbine. Photographed at Camden. This side of the engine was generally considered to be better looking than the other!/*P. Ransome-Wallis*

Right: The reverse turbine proved to be a troublesome feature, and was the cause of a number of failures in service. Much smaller than the forward turbines, it was intended for slow speed running only, and was normally used only when the engine was running light or shunting. It proved too small to allow the engine to push its empty stock up Camden bank to the carriage sidings outside Euston. In view of this, the illustration now reproduced is all the more remarkable as it shows No 6202 running tender-first on the up main-line at Bushey with a nine coach load. The reasons for this highly unusual operation are not known./*E.R. Wethersett*

Below right: The 'Turbomotive' inevitably paid the price of being a one-off experiment. Turbine failures were likely to involve a visit to works for rectification by experts, and time was often wasted whilst special replacement parts were obtained. On the credit side, the locomotive put up many splendid performances in everyday service and it was generally well-liked by enginemen once they had grown accustomed to its unusual features. In the hectic early war years this specialised machine was stored out of service at Crewe, but was reinstated in 1942. When again out of service in 1943 (as a result of turbine damage) its unique boiler was used on No 6210. The illustration shows No 6202 under repair at Crewe whilst still fitted with the original domeless boiler./*Photomatic*

signed by man'. He went on to say that: 'It has the poise, the rhythm and the balance reminiscent of some magnificent ship. This engine probably represents the apex of the pre-streamlined age'.

Intensive early trials were carried out on the Anglo-Scottish services, in comparison with the 'Princess Royals', but for the majority of its life, the locomotive was employed on the Euston-Liverpool run.

The experiment came to an end when the locomotive required extensive renewals including a new main turbine, which would have

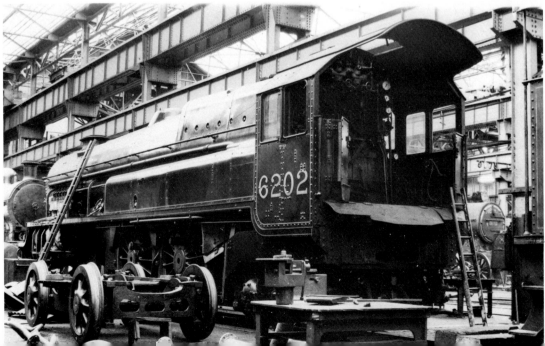

involved considerable expense. The decision was therefore taken to rebuild her conventionally. As BR No 46202, and named for the first time, *Princess Anne* (thus becoming the 'Princess Anne' type; *not* a 'Princess Royal'), she emerged from Crewe in the summer of 1952. A 'new' Stanier locomotive produced under BR auspices, with a handsome appearance. In her new form the locomotive was destined to have a tragically short career. Less than three months in service, she was one of the locomotives involved in the Harrow disaster. Damage was sufficiently severe to warrant withdrawal, although the boiler was repaired and used again.

Rebuilt: 1952
Withdrawn: 1954

Below: Trouble was experienced with the soft turbine exhaust drifting in front of the cab windows and as a result No 6202 was the first LMSR Pacific to receive smoke-deflectors, in 1939. This postwar view of the 'Turbomotive' shows the extended casing of the right hand reverse turbine, which housed a Worthington reciprocating oil pump, fitted in 1942. In this final condition the locomotive had a 40-element superheater, with triple elements, which increased the superheated surface to 832 sq ft. A novel feature of the locomotive was the manner in which it quietly moved along; seemingly effortless./*R. Whitfield*

Right: Running and repair costs rose sharply during the difficult war years and the immediate postwar years, and although acknowledged as a most worthwhile experiment it was decided to rebuild the locomotive as a conventional Pacific. As BR No 46202 *Princess Anne* she emerged from Crewe in August 1952, and is seen here at Euston on 28 August 1952, ready to work the 8.30am train to Liverpool. The front end layout resembled the 'Coronation' Pacifics, rather than the 'Princess Royals', and the engine was therefore designated the 'Princess Anne' type. It only ran 11,443 miles before it was damaged beyond economic repair in the Harrow disaster of October 1952./*BR*

Below right: The drawing shows incorrect front end cutaway to footplating ahead of outside cylinders.

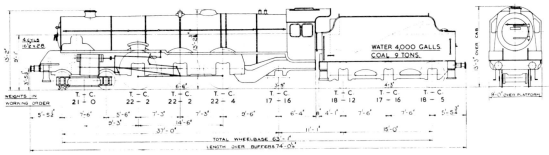

SECTION 7

2-8-0 Class 8F
Heavy Freight Engines
Introduced: 1935
Total: 852

Although Fowler had produced some 2-8-0s for the Somerset and Dorset Joint Railway, which later became part of the LMSR locomotive stock, these heavy freight engines designed by Stanier were the first really modern locomotives of that wheel arrangement to operate over the lines of the constituent companies of the LMSR.

The provision of a heavy goods engine had been under review since 1923 but the first design built was the rather unsatisfactory 7F 0-8-0 of Fowler design, introduced in 1929. In the 1933 programme five 2-8-0s were included (the Nos 13811-15 were allotted), but these were cancelled and replaced in the 1934 programme by two 'experimental' 2-8-0s to gain experience with heavy goods locomotives.

In the event, the initial batch was of 12 locomotives and these had domeless taper boilers, and these were at first classified 7F. All later examples had improved boilers, with separate dome and top feed, and were classified 8F; of the first 12, only No 8003 was brought into line with the rest, in order to provide a spare domeless boiler for the rest of the batch.

The original boilers had a total evaporative heating surface of 1,463sq ft, comprising a tube heating surface of 1,308sq ft and a firebox heating surface of 155sq ft. The superheater heating surface was 230sq ft, and the grate area was 27.8sq ft. The modified boilers later

introduced had the sloping throatplate, and the principal dimensions are listed below.

Two outside cylinders, 18½in by 28in, and Walschaerts long-travel valve gear were employed. The front Bissel truck had a radius bar 6ft 7¾in long, and wheels of 3ft 3½in diameter. The design of the locomotive in general followed the standard practices developed by Stanier, and the tenders were the standard 4,000 gallon, 9ton, capacity design with high curved sides.

One interesting feature of Nos 8000-11 was that they were not fitted with vacuum brake equipment, unlike the rest of class.

These engines soon proved their worth in everyday service on the LMSR, and it was not surprising that the design should be chosen by the War Department for quantity production to meet the urgent needs of World War 2 transportation; in the same way that the Robinson 2-8-0s of the Great Central Railway had been adopted for WD use in World War 1. As a result of this, the history of the 8Fs is very complex, and the ultimate fate of some

Top right: First of the class, No 8000, with domeless taper boiler: photographed in shop grey livery. Original power classification was 7F./*BR*

Right: No 8269 with a lengthy train of empty mineral wagons en route for Toton, passing Napsbury, in April 1948./*E.D. Bruton*

Heating surface, tubes
  Large and small: 1,479.0sq ft
  Firebox: 171.0sq ft
Total (evaporative): 1,650.0sq ft
Superheater: 245.0sq ft
  Superheater elements: 21
Combined heating surfaces: 1,895.0sq ft
Grate area: 28.65sq ft
Tractive effort (at 85 per cent BP): 32,438lb

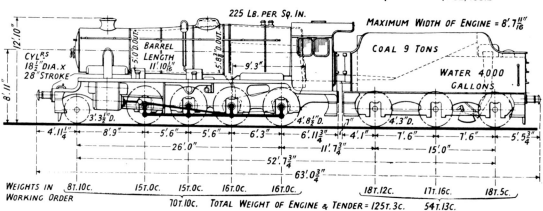

225 LB. PER SQ. IN.

MAXIMUM WIDTH OF ENGINE = 8'.7 11/16"

12'.10"

CYLRS 18½" DIA. X 28" STROKE

BARREL LENGTH 11'.10 1/16"

5'.0 D.OUT.

5'.8 3/8 D.OUT.

9'.3"

COAL 9 TONS

WATER 4,000 GALLONS

8'.11"

3'.3½" D.

4'.8½" D.

7"

4'.3" D.

4'.11¼" — 8'.9" — 5'.6" — 5'.6" — 6'.3" — 6'.11¾" — 4'.1" — 7'.6" — 7'.6" — 5'.5¾"

26'.0"

11'.7¾"

15'.0"

52'.7¾"

63'.0¾"

WEIGHTS IN WORKING ORDER   8T.10C.   15T.0C.   15T.0C.   16T.0C.   16T.0C.   18T.12C.   17T.16C.   18T.5C.

70T.10C.   TOTAL WEIGHT OF ENGINE & TENDER = 125T.3C.   54T.13C.

locomotives is uncertain. The War Department took over some engines from existing LMSR stock, and placed orders for further new batches. Of these, some were incorporated into LMSR stock, others were pure WD-owned and never carried LMSR running numbers. The total number constructed was 852, of which 133 were pure WD. This makes this the largest Stanier class; although only 668 in fact operated on British soil after the war.

It was at first envisaged that the WD locos would be used on the Continent of Europe, and those batches ordered specially were to have Flaman speed recorders, cab signalling apparatus and Westinghouse air brakes. However, the retreat to Dunkirk put an end to this plan, and in the event, the WD 8Fs went much further afield and saw operation in various parts of the Middle East, including Egypt, Turkey and Iran. Later some went to Italy for a while. Various renumberings took place (and several exchanged identities into the bargain). Most of those sent overseas by the WD were converted for oil-burning.

Of the locomotives taken over from LMSR stock by the WD, and those specially constructed, many were destined never to return to Britain.

Some were lost in transit when the ships carrying them were sunk to the bottom; some became almost complete wrecks through severe usage or neglect. The Egyptian State Railways, the Turkish State Railways, the Italian Railways, the Persian Railways and the Iraqi State Railways all took 8Fs into their permanent stock. Some examples are still running in Turkey, where they have the nickname 'Churchills'. It would be impossible in the space available to list all their various wanderings and re-numberings, but the general details of the class are as follows:

| Nos 8000-8011 | Crewe | 1935 |
| Nos 8012-8014 | Crewe | 1936 |

Below: Swindon-built 8F No 8457 on an up goods by Sonning Box. No smokebox numberplate fitted; GWR style numbers on bufferbeam./*M.W. Earley*

Right: Eastleigh-built 8F No 8661 seen when new, at Bournemouth East Goods Yard on the up 2.50pm Bevois Park goods workings; 1 July, 1944./*G.O.P. Pearce*

Below right: LNER Stanier 8F No 3548 (ex-3148) built at Doncaster in 1945 and seen here at York in July 1947, being coaled. Note 'Heaton' shed painted on bufferbeam, also LNER class '06'./*C.C.B. Herbert*

Nos 8015-8026	Crewe	1937
Nos 8027-8095	Vulcan Foundry	1936/37
Nos 8096-8097	Crewe	1938
Nos 8098-8125	Crewe	1939
Nos 8126-8139	Crewe	1941
Nos 8140-8157	Crewe	1942
Nos 8158-8175	Crewe	1943
Nos 8176-8225	North British	1942

Of the above, 51 were requisitioned by the WD, and only 11 of these were returned in due course. Four were lost in transit.

When not needed for service in France, the WD order was cut down from 240 to 100 and all were allotted LMSR numbers 8226-8235, but only Nos 8226-8263 and 8286-8300 worked in Britain, several being lent to the GWR, then in urgent need of heavy goods engines.

Nos 8226-8263	North British	1940

All these were taken over by the WD in 1941 and shipped abroad (as WD Nos 300-37). Two were lost in transit. (The locomotives that were returned from the WD to BR as Nos 48246-48263 were not the original locomotives allocated these numbers.)

Nos 8264-8285	North British	1942

(WD Nos 549-51/3/5-71, 623).

At first allocated to the WD, but placed in LMSR stock in 1943. Two other engines, also built at this time, were shipped to Turkey and never given LMSR numbers. (WD Nos 552/4).

Nos 8286-8300	Beyer Peacock	1940

(WD Nos 400-15).

Taken over by the WD in 1941, and shipped abroad. One was lost in transit. No 8293 was involved in an accident at Slough, whilst on loan to the GWR in 1941, and was not shipped with the rest. It was actually withdrawn but was reinstated within a week and returned to LMSR stock after repair. (The locomotives returned by the WD to BR as their Nos 48286-48292 and 48294-48297 were not those which originally carried those numbers, although four had originally been numbered in this group).

Nos 8301-8316	Crewe	1943
Nos 8317-8330	Crewe	1944
Nos 8331-8337	Horwich	1943
Nos 8338-8381	Horwich	1944
Nos 8382-8399	Horwich	1945
Nos 8400-8426	Swindon	1943
Nos 8427-8448	Swindon	1944
Nos 8449-8479	Swindon	1945

The Swindon built locomotives were on loan to the GWR from new. They were handed over to the LMSR in 1946/7.

Nos 8480-8489	*Not used.*	
Nos 8490-8495	Horwich	1945

These locomotives introduced the rocking grate and self-cleaning smokebox to the LMSR.

Nos 8496-8499	*Not used.*	
Nos 8500-8509	Darlington	1944
Nos 8510-8525	Doncaster	1944

Left: WD No 70441 being shipped at Port Said for service in Italy; using a Suez Canal Co, 150 ton floating crane./*K.R.M. Cameron*

Top right: Morning express from Beirut to Haifa, at Beirut Yard with WD No 70596 (oil-burning). Note enlarged top feed casing. Picture taken in 1944. The coaches are G.I.P. Rly (India) converted from broad to standard gauge./*K.R.M. Cameron*

Right: Running with an Austerity 8-wheeled tender. No M8602 is seen at Euston on empty coaching stock in June 1948./*H.C. Casserley*

Nos 8526-8539	Doncaster	1945
Nos 8540-8542	Darlington	1944
Nos 8543-8559	Darlington	1945

All the Doncaster and Darlington built locomo-

tives were on loan to the LNER from new, and were handed over to the LMSR in 1946/7.

| Nos 8560-8599 | *Not used.* | |
| Nos 8600-8601 | Eastleigh | 1942 |

Nos 8602-8609	Eastleigh	1943
Nos 8610-8612	Ashford	1943
Nos 8613-8617	Brighton	1943
Nos 8618-8624	Ashford	1943
Nos 8625-8649	Brighton	1943
Nos 8650-8660	Eastleigh	1943
Nos 8661-8662	Eastleigh	1944
Nos 8663-8670	Brighton	1944
No 8671	Ashford	1943
Nos 8672-8674	Ashford	1944
Nos 8675-8678	Brighton	1944
Nos 8679-8680	Brighton	1943
Nos 8681-8704	Brighton	1944

The above locomotives, built in Southern Railway workshops, were intended for service on the LMSR although some ran on the SR when new. In addition to these, the SR built some further 8Fs for the LNER (see note below). These had slight modifications and were allocated LNER numbers, as follows:

| LNER Nos 7651-7675 | Brighton | 1944 |

These were later renumbered LNER Nos 3100-3124, and later still became Nos 3500-3524 (LNER class O6). They were handed over to the LMSR in 1946/7 and became Nos 8705-8729.

Further 8Fs were built for the LNER, as follows:

| LNER Nos 3125-3147 | Darlington | 1945/6 |

These were renumbered LNER Nos 3525-3547 (class O6) and became LMSR Nos 8730-8752 when handed over in 1946/7.

| LNER Nos 3148-3167 | Doncaster | 1945/6 |

These became LNER Nos 3548-3567 (class O6)

and were returned to the LMSR as their Nos 8753-8772, in 1946/7 except No 3554 (8759), in 1948.

The LNER agreed 'in the National Interest' to accept engines of LMSR design, when pressed to do so by the Ministry of War Transport, 100 being authorised but only the 68 listed were built. At one stage the LNER engines were to have LMS numbers, which would have filled the blanks (except Nos 8480-9 which were allotted to engines to be built at Swindon, but which were cancelled) and this would have taken the list up to No 8706.

In addition to the above locomotives, which carried LMSR numbers at some stage in their careers, the following 8Fs were built to WD order:

| WD Nos 338-339 | North British | 1941 |

Below: One of the series built for the War Department is seen in postwar service in the Middle East. Iraqi State Railways oil-burning Stanier 2-8-0 No 1428, leaving Baiji with a freight for Baghdad, in 1952. The engine has a capuchon added to the chimney and carries a large electric headlight. A four-wheeled auxiliary water tender is attached./*P. J. Bawcutt*

Right: In 1956, some Swindon-built 8Fs were transferred back to the Western Region, to replace withdrawn ex-ROD 2-8-0s. They were easily distinguishable by the modified ejector pipe on the left hand side of the boiler. No 48402 makes a fine picture as it lifts a coal train up the bank to Filton Junction, Bristol in December 1957; assisted in the rear by a 2-6-2T./*G.F. Heiron*

Below right: Three more 8Fs were returned to BR stock in 1957 after a period of WD service in this country. They became Nos 48773-48775, and were overhauled at Eastleigh before entering BR service. No 48774 is shown at Polmadie shed on February 17, 1962. Note the non-standard top feed casing which betrays the WD origin./*D.C. Smith*

WD Nos 415-449   Beyer Peacock   1941
WD Nos 500-524   North British   1941
WD Nos 540-548   North British   1941/2
(The full WD number range was Nos 300-449, 500-524, 540-571 and 623, with requisitioned LMSR engines renumbered WD 572-622)

Five WD locomotives were returned from Egypt in 1952, for repair at Derby and instead of being sent back they then went to the Longmoor Military Railway in 1955. Of these, three were returned to BR stock in 1957 as Nos 48773-5. One was in fact the eleventh ex-LMSR engine No 8025, but was not recognised as such, otherwise it would doubtless have become No 48025. The other two were sent to the Cairnryan Military Railway in Scotland.

A little known development of the Stanier 8F design was the production of what might be termed 'half' Stanier 2-8-0s for Egypt around 1952. Very satisfied with the 8Fs that they had

taken into their own stock, the ESR ordered considerable numbers of additional locomotives built new by Continental and British manufacturers. In these orders, the chassis was identical with that of the Stanier engines, but a different parallel-boiler was applied using flanging blocks standard with other Egyptian classes.

In Iraq a similar thing happened when new engines were obtained from Germany, having a much larger boiler on Stanier frames. A letter to the November 1980 issue of *Railway World* revealed that six Class 8Fs still exist in Iran, at a dump at Ahwaz. These are ex-LMSR Nos 8013/4/30 and WD Nos 362/543/5. Efforts are being made to preserve one or more of these and return them to Britain.

First of class withdrawn (BR stock): 48616 (1960)
Last of class withdrawn (BR stock): 48773 (1968)
Examples preserved: 48151, 48431, 48773

Left: In the late 1950s an exchange of tenders took place between the 8Fs and some 'Jubilee' class 4-6-0s. The Stanier tenders were given to the Jubilees and their Fowler 3,500 gallon narrow tenders were paired with the 8Fs. No 48045 (one of the locomotives returned from the Middle East) was photographed with a Fowler tender, at Northwich, 15 March, 1959./*K.R. Pirt*

Bottom left: Nearing the end of its career on BR, but destined to be saved by enthusiasts (see page 121) No 48773 (formerly WD Nos 70307/500) at Bolton in June 1968. Diagonal cabside stripe denotes it was prohibited south of Crewe under the wires and the star painted below the number denotes that it had 50 per cent of the reciprocating

weights balanced, to enable it to run on fast freight duties./*John A.M. Vaughan*

Above: BR No 48115 poses on the turntable at Patricroft shed in August 1961./*J.R. Carter*

Below: Turkish 8F No 45161 (WD No 522) alongside US-built 2-10-0 No 56355 in 1970./*R.G. Farr*

Bottom: Close-up of Turkish 8F No 45168 (WD No 340) looking somewhat the worse for wear; at Irmak in 1970. Detail alterations include lid to chimney, modified top feed, pilot (cowcatcher) and cutaway footplating ahead of cylinders. Air-brakes fitted./*R.G. Farr*

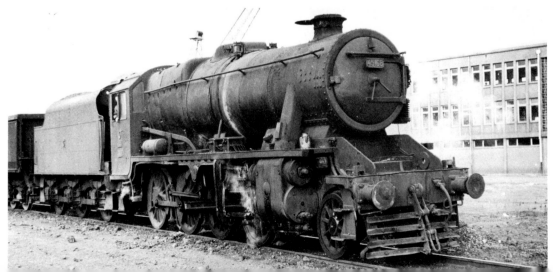

2-6-4T Class 4P
Passenger Tank Engines
Introduced: 1935
Total: 206

As already mentioned in Section 5, the 3-cylinder 2-6-4T design introduced by Stanier for the Southend line in 1934 had not demonstrated any marked advantage over the earlier Fowler 2-cylinder engines when used on similar duties. Stanier was quick to realise the significance of this in terms of cost and weight per locomotive, and the following year saw the introduction of the first of his 2-cylinder version of the taper boiler 2-6-4T.

The initial batch of eight locomotives had low-degree superheat domeless taper boilers, but all subsequent engines had boilers of improved design, with separate dome and top feed and No 2538 of the first batch was modified to take this boiler. As first introduced, the domeless boiler had a barrel identical to that provided for the 3-cylinder engines, with a working pressure of 200lbs per sq in. The total heating surface was 1,168sq ft. Tractive effort at 85 per cent of the working pressure was 24,670lb. The later, improved, boiler with dome, is dimensionally detailed at the end of this section.

The coal bunker was arranged to be as self-trimming as possible, and the top was angled inwards towards the rear end in order to improve vision when running bunker first. Water pick-up gear was fitted between the rear coupled wheels and the leading wheels of the trailing bogie, and could be used when the locomotive was running either chimney first or bunker first.

These handsome locomotives were widely distributed over the LMSR system and proved to be excellent performers. In many places they were known as the 'Derby Tanks'.

Right: One of the initial batch of eight Derby-built locomotives, with domeless taper boiler. No 42544 was photographed leaving the cutting near Shap Cummit with the down 5pm Oxenholme–Carlisle stopping train composed of Eastern Region Stock; 3 June, 1950./E.D. Bruton

Bottom right: No 2449, with the later, improved standard taper boiler with separate dome and top feed. Seen here leaving Bushey with a Euston–Bletchley train./P. Ransome-Wallis

Heating surface, tubes
  Large and small: 1,223.0sq ft
  Firebox: 143.0sq ft
Total (evaporative): 1,366.0sq ft
Superheater: 245.0sq ft
  Superheater elements: 21
Combined heating surfaces: 1,611.0sq ft
Grate area: 26.7sq ft
Tractive effort (at 85 per cent BP): 24,670lb

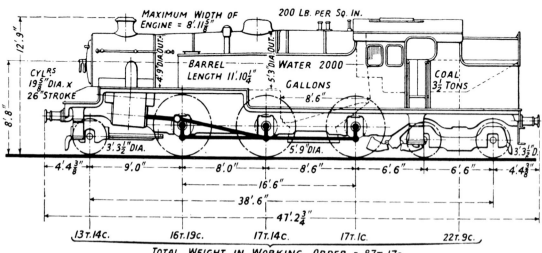

MAXIMUM WIDTH OF ENGINE = 8'.11⅝"

200 LB. PER SQ. IN.

12'.9"

4'.9"DIA.OUT.

5'.3"DIA.OUT.

BARREL LENGTH 11'.10¼"

WATER 2000 GALLONS

CYLRS 19⅝"DIA. X 26"STROKE

COAL 3½ TONS

8'.8"

8'.6"

3'.3½"DIA.

5'.9"DIA.

3'.3½"D.

4'.4⅜" — 9'.0" — 8'.0" — 8'.6" — 6'.6" — 6'.6" — 4'.4⅜"

16'.6"

38'.6"

47'.2¾"

13T.14C.   16T.19C.   17T.14C.   17T.1C.   22T.9C.

TOTAL WEIGHT IN WORKING ORDER = 87T. 17C.

The engines were built as follows:

Nos 2425-2475	Derby	1936
Nos 2476-2494	Derby	1937
Nos 2537-2544	Derby	1935
Nos 2545-2609	North British	1936
Nos 2610-2617	North British	1937
Nos 2618-2651	Derby	1938
No 2652	Derby	1939
No 2653	Derby	1940
Nos 2654-2662	Derby	1941
Nos 2663-2670	Derby	1942
Nos 2671-2672	Derby	1943

First of class withdrawn: 42490 (1960)
Last of class withdrawn: 42616 (1967)
None preserved

Below: Familiar companions; but photographed at a strange location. The 2-6-4Ts were used for London area inter-regional workings in BR days. No 42430 is seen here at East Croydon on 25 May, 1963 having just arrived with a parcels train from Willesden Junction. By coincidence, another LMR loco, double-chimney class 5 4-6-0 No 44766 is also present, taking water *en route* to the South Coast with an excursion train./*Author*

Right: An impressive combination of Stanier steam power, 2-cylinder 2-6-4T No 42464 assists 'Princess Royal' class Pacific No 46203 *Princess Margaret Rose,* with the 11.15am Birmingham–Glasgow express, seen passing Scout Green on 26 January, 1957. The 2-6-4T assisted from Oxenholme to Shap Summit./*J.E. Wilkinson*

Below right: Working bunker first, Class 4P 2-6-4T No 42613 pilots 'Jubilee' Class 5XP 4-6-0 No 45717 *Dauntless* on a Liverpool–Windermere train at Oxenholme on 31 August, 1963./*D. Cross*

Nos 145-165	Derby	1937
Nos 166-184	Derby	1938
Nos 185-190	Crewe	1937
Nos 191-209	Crewe	1938

Nos 71-144 were built domeless but Nos 121-144 had boilers with the longer grate. The remainder of the class were delivered new with modified

2-6-2T Class 3P
Passenger Tank Engines
Introduced: 1935
Total: 139

Basically this was a taper boiler version of the Fowler 2-6-2T design of 1930, with detail improvements, but retaining the same general dimensions. This small tank engine design is generally considered to have been the least satisfactory of the range of standard types produced by Stanier. Somewhat under-boilered, the class had a reputation as indifferent performers and, although improvements were subsequently made, nothing succeeded in altering this in the eyes of the enginemen.

The design in general followed the conventions established during the Stanier regime, with a domeless taper boiler with top feed, and with an excellent cab design. The coal bunker was carried higher than the rear cab windows, and was angled inwards between them, to provide a good look-out when running bunker first. The bunker was arranged to be as self-trimming as possible.

The engines were built as follows:

| Nos 71-144 | Derby | 1935 |

Right: One of the 1935 Derby-built batch, in original condition with domeless taper boiler. This had low degree superheat. When new the class was finished in black livery with red lining. No 99 is depicted in ex-works condition, at St Pancras./*P. Ransome-Wallis*

Below right: The second series was constructed in 1937/8 at both Derby and Crewe. The main difference was the improved boiler design, with separate top feed and steam dome except on Nos 121-144, which were domeless. Trials held in attempts to improve the draughting resulted in the adoption, as standard, of a modernised version of the Adams 'Vortex' blastpipe, with larger diameter chimney. No 40149 is shown with all these features, working a St Pancras surburban duty past Elstree./*F. R. Hebron*

Heating surface, tubes
  Large and small: 996.4sq ft
  Firebox: 111.2sq ft
Total (evaporative): 1,107.6sq ft
Superheater: 145.0sq ft
  Superheater elements: 14
Combined heating surfaces: 1,252.6sq ft
Grate area: 19.2sq ft
Tractive effort (at 85 per cent BP): 21,486lb

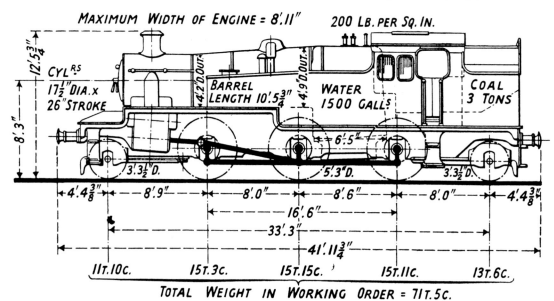

Left: The larger diameter chimney used in conjunction with the 'Vortex' blastpipe is very apparent in this view of No 40072, at Blackpool. The engine retains the original domeless taper boiler. Nos 83, 87, 114 and 139 were altered to take the later type of boiler, in order to provide spares for the remainder of the class with domeless boilers./*A. Swain*

Bottom left: The larger boiler, tried out soon after the beginning of World War 2. This had a total heating surface of 1,106sq ft, with a 14-element superheater providing 145sq ft. The tubes provided 995sq ft and the firebox 111sq ft. Grate area was increased to 19.2sq ft. All this was achieved with an increase in locomotive weight of only 1¼ tons. No 40167 is seen here on empty stock at St Pancras./*A. Swain*

Below: Class 3P 2-6-2T No 40181 pilots Ivatt Class 2 2-6-0 No 46443 on the 3.10pm Chinley–Sheffield, at Chinley North Junction on 7 September, 1957./*E. Oldham*

Bottom: In spotless lined-black livery, No 40071, photographed at Stockport Edgeley on 1 June, 1957./ *T. Lewis*

boilers, having separate dome top feed and longer grate.

They were used on a variety of stopping train, branch line, empty stock and banking duties, and examples of the class were allocated to most parts of the LMSR system at various times in their career.

In a final attempt to improve upon their indifferent performance, more drastic rebuilding was contempated soon after the beginning of World War 2, when a larger boiler was tried out. This did not prove to be worth the money, and only six engines of the class carried the larger boilers; Nos 142/148/163/167/169/203.

First of class withdrawn
(small boiler)—40139(1959)
(large boiler)—40169 (1959)
Last of class withdrawn:
(small boiler)—40196 (1962)
(large boiler)—40148 (1962)
None preserved

4-6-0 Class 6P
(BR Power Class 7P)
Express Passenger Engine
Introduced: 1935
Total: 1
'Royal Scot'

Although listed as one of the 'Royal Scot' class, No 6170 *British Legion* was in certain important respects a unique locomotive.

Following a tragic failure whilst still on trial in Scotland, the Fowler experimental high pressure 4-6-0 No 6399 *Fury,* had been little used since 1930. For some years the damaged engine was stored in the paint shop at Derby, making only occasional runs, and it was the decision to rebuild it as a conventional 4-6-0, utilising certain parts such as the frames and wheels of the original, that resulted in the appearance of No 6170 in 1935.

It would perhaps be more accurate to describe *British Legion* as Stanier's *equivalent* to the original 'Royal Scot' design, rather than as a conversion. In fact it incorporated the standard features of Stanier's practice, and in addition it demonstrated many improvements upon the earlier Stanier 4-6-0s, particularly in the design of the taper boiler which, as early as 1932 was planned for use on Fowler's 'Royal Scot' class. This had a separate dome and top feed, and a working pressure of 250lb per sq in. As first built, the boiler had a total heating surface of 1,864sq ft, comprising tube heating surface of 1,669sq ft; firebox heating surface of 195sq ft; superheater heating surface of 360sq ft, and grate area of 31.25sq ft. The boiler was modified during the course of the engine's life and its later principal dimensions are listed below.

The main point which made this engine unique was the boiler, with a distance between tubeplates of 14ft 3in compared to 13ft 0in for the Converted 'Royal Scot' class. There was no spare boiler, and visits to works for heavy repair tended to be rather lengthy, as a result.

In common with the Fowler engines a 3-cylinder layout was used, with Walschaerts long-travel valve gear, but the cylinders were modified to provide a saddle for the smokebox. When new there was a crosshead vacuum pump located on the left-hand side.

In prewar days No 6170 was allocated to Longsight, later it was transferred to Camden, and in its final years to Crewe North. However for a while in 1943-4 it worked from Leeds, with the first of the 'Converted Scots'.

The locomotive was constructed at Crewe.

Withdrawn: 1962.

Below: Showing original layout of outside steampipes; raked back.

Heating surface, tubes
  Large and small: 1,793.0sq ft
  Firebox: 195.0sq ft
Total (evaporative): 195.0sq ft
Superheater: 392.0sq ft
  Superheater elements: 28
Combined heating surfaces: 2,380.0
Grate area: 31.25sq ft
Tractive effort (at 85 per cent BP): 33,150lb

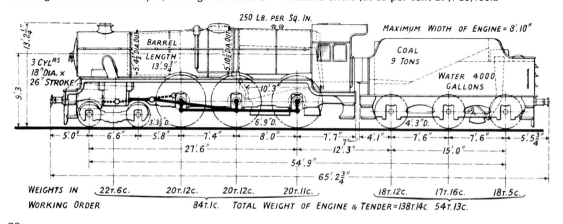

Top: As first built, No 6170 *British Legion* had a single blastpipe and chimney. The taper boiler had the top feed immediately ahead of the dome. An early modification was made to the outside steam pipes, which were at first raked back. No 6170 was the only taper boilered 'Royal Scot' to receive LMSR crimson lake livery, and the only engine of the class to have a Stanier side-window cab. The tender was of standard 4,000 gallon Stanier high sided design, with 9 tons coal capacity./E. Treacy

Above: Steaming at first proved erratic, and a Kylchap double blastpipe and chimney were later fitted, and modifications made to the cylinders, with satisfactory results. No 46170 is seen here in postwar LMSR black livery, but with BR number and lettering. Photographed climbing Camden Bank with the 4.5pm express to Holyhead; 22 May, 1949./C.C.B. Herbert

Below: In final state, with smoke deflectors added, No 46170 is seen in ex-works condition at Crewe; in BR green livery./J.R. Carter

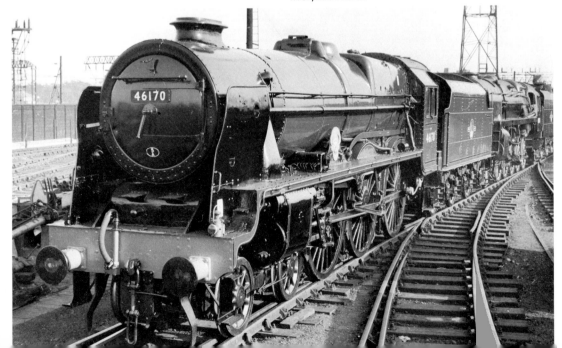

SECTION 11

4-6-2 Class 7P
(BR Power Class 8P)
Express Passenger Engines
Introduced: 1937
Total: 38
'Princess Coronation' or 'Duchess'

By the mid 1930s the competition from road and air, and from the rival LNER services, made some speeding-up of the principal express trains highly desirable. Plans were therefore put in hand for a new high-speed Anglo-Scottish train, to be introduced in Coronation year 1937; also for a general increase in the number of trains running to 'XL' schedules.

Although the 'Princess Royals' were performing well on the Anglo-Scottish run it was realised that an improved Pacific design was needed, with a built-in capacity for sustained high-speed steaming. The importance of internally streamlined steam passages had been recognised by

André Chapelon, and Stanier took full advantage of this advance in locomotive engineering when scheming-out his new Pacific. Particular attention was paid to the front end layout, and careful tests were made to ensure the freest possible passage of steam into and out of the cylinders.

All vestiges of Stanier's early bias towards low-degree superheat had been swept aside by the time the 'Coronation' Pacifics were on the drawing-board, and with a 40-element superheater of 856sq ft, the new design had the largest superheating surface of any British locomotive. Compared to the 'Princess Royals', there were other important changes in the design. The boiler was vastly improved, with splendid steam-raising capacity, and the total evaporative

Heating surface, tubes
    Large and small: 2,577.0sq ft
    Firebox: 230.5sq ft
Total (evaporative): 2,807.5sq ft
Superheater: 856.0sq ft
    Superheater elements (triple): 40
Combined heating surfaces: 3,663.5sq ft
Grate area: 50.0sq ft
Tractive effort (at 85 per cent BP): 40,000lb

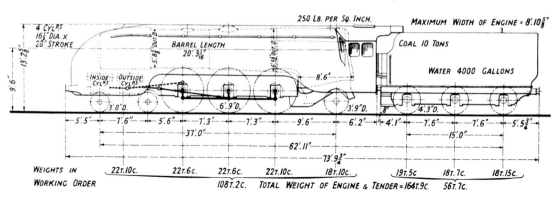

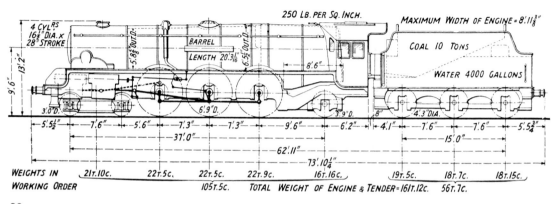

80

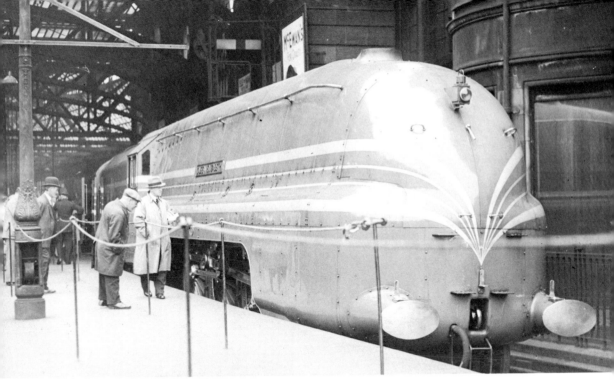

Above: 'Princess Coronation' Pacific No 6221 *Queen Elizabeth* on show at Glasgow Central before going into service./*F.R. Hebron*

Left: First of the 'Princess Coronation' class. Blue and silver liveried No 6220 *Coronation* streaks through the countryside near Watford with the inaugural 'Coronation Scot' train. This view emphasises the streamlined form adopted for the new Pacifics, which was the subject of considerable research./*Ian Allan Library*

heating surface was increased from 2,516 to 2,807sq ft. The driving wheel diameter was increased from 6ft 6in to 6ft 9in, and to prevent any significant loss of tractive effort as a result of the larger wheel diameter, the diameter of the cylinders was increased by ¼in. The outside cylinders were brought forward and all trace of the GWR 'King' class cylinder disposition, as used on the 'Princess Royals' disappeared. Only two sets of outside valve motion were used, with the inside valves worked by rocking-shafts from the outside valve spindle crossheads, (the inverse of Swindon practice, where the outside cylinder valves were operated by rocking-shafts from the inside cylinder valve motion set between the frames).

As first built the locomotives had a tube-heating surface of 2,577sq ft, a firebox heating surface of 230sq ft, making a total evaporative heating surface of 2,807sq ft. The superheater heating surface was 856sq ft (soon reduced to

830sq ft), and the grate area was no less than 50sq ft. Later dimensions are shown in the table below.

The new LNER streamliners had caught popular imagination, and thus it was hardly surprising that when the new series of Pacifics was planned for the LMSR it was agreed that the first of these should be finished in streamlined form. Of interest here is that Stanier was actually away in India, on a special committee whilst the detail design work was in hand. The decision to enclose the locomotive in an aerodynamical shroud resulted in approximately two extra tons of metal; the engine weight in working order being 108.1 tons. Over the years considerable debate has centred around the relative merits of streamlined versus conventional locomotive forms for engines intended to operate at high speeds, and a general conclusion is that the reduction in wind resistance only offsets the added weight when a really long continuous high-speed run is possible. Such conditions were hard to find in Britain in prewar days (consider the vast expenditure on civil engineering which preceded the introduction of today's 100mph electric service from Euston), and it is significant that removal of the streamlined casings from the 'Princess Coronation' Pacifics at a later stage in their career, did not apparently affect their everyday performance in the slightest. But in the 1930s the public craze was for streamlining, and from a publicity point of view, the Directors of the LMSR were undoubtedly wise in bowing to this.

Certainly the shape evolved at Derby was an eye-catching one, with a rich Caledonian blue livery offset by four bold silver cheat lines, which commenced in a chevron at the front of the locomotive and were carried horizontally along the sides. For the special high-speed train introduced in 1937, the 'Coronation Scot', the livery was continued down the entire length of the train. The visual effect of this, and the publicity gained from a maximum speed of 114mph, achieved by No 6220 *Coronation*, on a

Below: A dramatic view of No 6224 *Princess Alexandra* at speed past Willesden with the 'Coronation Scot' in February 1938./*E.R. Wethersett*

Right: With Nos 6230-6234 a superficial change took place, in that they were constructed without the streamlined outer casing. Many enthusiasts regarded these truly massive engines as the most handsome of Stanier's Pacifics. Illustrated in immaculate condition is No 6232 *Duchess of Montrose*, as originally built. In 1939, No 6234 of this non-streamlined batch was fitted with an experimental double blastpipe and chimney, and it was as a result of tests with this locomotive that all the 'Princess Coronation' Pacifics were subsequently given double chimneys./*E. Treacy*

Below right: This rear three-quarters view of No 6231 *Duchess of Atholl* emphasises the impressive appearance of the original non-streamlined Pacifics. Note the speedometer driven off the rear coupled driving wheels. The maroon livery applied to Nos 6230-6234 when new was of special high-quality finish, with gilt lining edged with vermilion./*P. Ransome-Wallis*

special test run, did much to restore prestige to the LMSR Anglo-Scottish service and took some of the limelight off the rival LNER streamliners.

Five locomotives were delivered in this form, and soon demonstrated that the design was an outstanding success. No modifications were necessary; the engines steamed and rode magnificently right from the start. Without doubt the 'Coronation' Pacific, the last new design by Stanier for the LMSR, was his masterpiece.

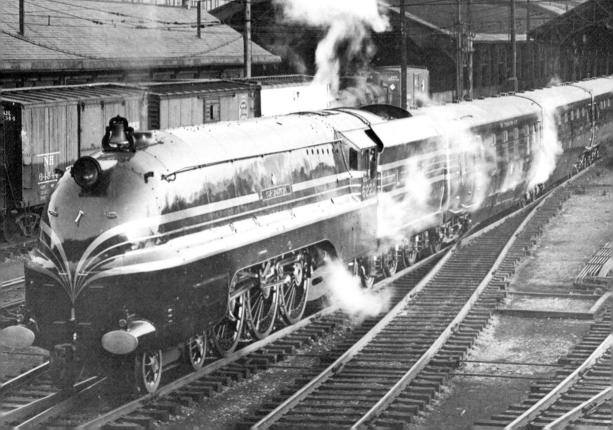

Above left: For the 1939 New York World's Fair, the LMSR shipped a 'Princess Coronation' Pacific and part of a new set of carriages intended for the 1940 'Coronation Scot' service. No 6229 *Duchess of Hamilton,* completed at Crewe in September 1938, exchanged identities with the original No 6220 *Coronation,* specially for this event. Seen here as No 6220, but in the maroon and gilt livery of the second streamlined series, (from No 6225 onwards) the locomotive is being unloaded at Baltimore, after shipment from Southampton./*Ian Allan Library*

Left: No 6229 alias 6220 *Coronation* made an extensive tour over American Railroads, from 21 March to 14 April 1939 (covering 3121 miles), prior to going on show at New York. To conform with American law, the engine was equipped with bell and large electric headlight. The train is seen here on Baltimore and Ohio metals at the commencement of the tour. The train was still in America when World War 2 broke out, and it was not until 1943 that it was considered safe to ship the locomotive back to Britain; the carriages remained in America until the war was over. *Coronation* was unloaded at Cardiff, and once back on LMSR metals it resumed its former identity as No 6229, and the real No 6220 once again became the first of the class./*Ian Allan Library*

Above: Further streamlined engines were constructed in 1939/40/3, despite the outbreak of World War 2. But by 1943 it was proving difficult to justify the added cost and weight involved. In addition, the lack of cleaners meant that all publicity value was gone; whilst the hard-pressed maintenance staff were justifiably critical of the added complications of servicing these machines, with many parts not readily accessible without time-wasting removal of portions of the streamlined casing. The final streamliners were painted plain black when new, and earlier ones were repainted black as they passed through works. Illustrated is No 6228 *Duchess of Rutland* showing all too clearly the effects of austerity conditions as the camera catches her passing Berkhamsted in September 1946./*H.C. Casserley*

More of the class were required for the principal London-Scotland and London-Merseyside services, to operate 'XL' schedules, and the next batch were also streamlined, but the livery was changed to maroon and gilt. The probable reason for this was the closer match it made to normal LMSR maroon carriages, when the locomotives were used on services other than the 'Coronation Scot' (which it was intended should also be repainted in maroon and gilt in due course).

It seems that the passion for streamlining had cooled off by 1938, for the next batch to appear were not streamlined—and very handsome they proved to be! The change was only superficial, no working parts were affected, but the weight was reduced to 106.4 tons. However, further streamlined locomotives appeared next, and it was not until the changed conditions of wartime operation and maintenance made such frivolities appear decidedly out of place, that further non-streamlined Pacifics were built.

Principal allocations of the class were always to Camden, Crewe, Carlisle, Polmadie and Edge Hill, and their spheres of activity were the Euston-Glasgow, Euston-Liverpool and Crewe-Perth runs. They were also to be found on the Perth-Aberdeen, Carlisle-Glasgow St Enoch runs, and at Edinburgh Princes Street; sometimes they were to be seen on the North Wales coast. They were the obvious choice for Royal Train duties over the West Coast route and were always beautifully groomed for this honour; although in prewar days there was something faintly ludicrous about the spectacle of a streamlined blue and silver Pacific at the head of the majestic clerestory carriages finished in LNWR plum and spilt milk livery.

The tender design was based upon the high-capacity 4,000 gallon version finally fitted to the 'Princess Royals' with a coal capacity of 10 tons. These had proved slightly troublesome on the through Anglo-Scottish workings, as the coal farthest from the footplate was difficult to fetch forward by hand. For the 'Princess Coronation' Pacifics, Stanier introduced a steam-operated mechanical coal pusher, which greatly eased the fireman's task. The tenders for the streamlined engines had extended side sheets and the frames and bearing springs were partially concealed by a valance. A major change, given a considerable amount of thought, about 1955, but not implemented was the idea of fitting a mechanical stoker and an enlarged eight-wheeled tender (carring 12 tons of coal and 5000 gallons of water, and weighing 66 tons).

The engines were built as follows:

| Nos 6220-6224 | Crewe | 1937 |

Streamlined. Blue and silver livery.

| Nos 6225-6229 | Crewe | 1938 |

Streamlined. Maroon and gilt livery.

| Nos 6230-6234 | Crewe | 1938 |

Non-streamlined. Maroon and gilt livery.

| Nos 6235-6239 | Crewe | 1939 |
| Nos 6240-6244 | Crewe | 1940 |

Streamlined. Maroon and gilt livery.

| Nos 6245-6248 | Crewe | 1943 |

Streamlined. Wartime black livery.

| Nos 6249-6252 | Crewe | 1944 |

Non-streamlined. Wartime black livery.

| Nos 6253-6255 | Crewe | 1946 |

Non-streamlined. Postwar LMSR black livery.

| No 6256 | Crewe | 1947 |
| No 46257 | Crewe | 1948 |

Non-streamlined. Postwar LMSR black livery (46257 was lettered 'British Railways'). Modified design by H. G. Ivatt.

The liveries denoted above are those carried by the various batches when new.

First of class withdrawn: 46227/31/2 (1962)
Last of class withdrawn: 46256 (1964)
Examples preserved: 46229/33/5

Top left: Nos 6249-6252, built in 1944, reverted to the non-streamlined form of Nos 6230-6234. Their tenders were however, streamlined as this batch Nos 6235-54 were ordered as streamliners. No 6250 *City of Lichfield* is shown as first delivered, in wartime black livery. Commencing with No 6235 all the new Pacifics were built with double chimneys (on No 6245 this was an experimental Kylchap version), and the earlier engines were similarly modified./*BR*

Bottom left: As already mentioned, wartime conditions had drawn attention to the maintenance problems created by the streamlined casings, and in order to permit more ready access for maintenance, it was decided to remove the casings from all the locomotives concerned. This involved the provision of new platforms, but with the gap shown at the front end to give access to the outside cylinder valves, unlike those built without the streamline casing, (and No 46242 after repair following the 1952 Harrow collision). A most striking feature of the de-streamlined Pacifics was the tapered top to the smokebox. These smokeboxes had been tailored to suit the streamlined form, and they were retained until they became life expired. The first Pacific to be de-streamlined was No 6235 *City of Birmingham* in 1946. These modifications are clearly visible in this lovely study of No

46240 *City of Coventry* being prepared for a Royal Train duty. Smoke deflectors were added to the class after the war, and the tender had the streamlining removed./*BR*

Below: After the 1944 non-streamlined batch no further new Pacifics were constructed until 1946, when Nos 6253-6255 were delivered from Crewe. These were non-streamlined engines and had smoke-deflectors right from the start. The front end footplating was cut away in similar fashion to the de-streamlined engines. No 46255 *City of Hereford*, in BR blue livery, was photographed on a running-in turn in September 1950./*E. Treacy*

Bottom: The two final 'Princess Coronation' Pacifics, built in 1947/8, were to a modified design by H.G. Ivatt. Timken roller bearings were fitted to all axles on engine and tender, and the trailing truck was of one-piece cast steel construction. They had the new standard postwar features introduced by Ivatt; the rocking grate, self-emptying ashpan and self-cleaning smokebox, (these features were also on Nos 6253-6255 built in 1946). In this final form they represented the finest heavy express passenger power ever produced for a British railway. By a happy inspiration it was decided to name No 6256 *Sir William A. Stanier, FRS.* The engine carried electric lighting for some time./*BR*

Left: It was a de-streamlined 'Princess Coronation' Pacific that was chosen to represent the class in the 1948 Locomotive Exchanges. No 46236 *City of Bradford* is seen here on the Eastern Region. When running trials on the Southern it was necessary to couple an 8-wheel 'Austerity' tender (lettered LMS), because of the absence of water troughs on the SR./*E.R. Wethersett*

Below left: One of the original non-streamlined batch, No 46230 *Duchess of Buccleuch* as running in BR days, with double chimney and smoke-deflectors added. Photographed at Carlisle, waiting to take the down 'Royal Scot' forward to Glasgow./*E. Treacy*

Right: This unusual view of No 46238 *City of Carlisle,* photographed in Crewe North shed yard on 25 June 1964, emphasises the massive proportions of these handsome engines. It also clearly shows the cutaway footplating at the front end, and the double chimney. The tapered smokebox has been replaced by a new one of normal shape./*J.R. Carter*

Below: In 1955/6 comparative trials took place between the Stanier Pacific design and the WR 'King' class 4-6-0s, as modified by BR with larger superheater and double chimney. The 'Coronations' were represented by No 46237 *City of Bristol,* which ran on the 'Cornish Riviera' express with dynamometer car attached. The engine also ran over the Paddington–Birmingham route. Here No 46237 shows its paces between Newton Abbot and Teignmouth./ *D.S. Fish*

Above: Another shot of No 46238 *City of Carlisle,* taken as she headed a Carlisle United football supporters excursion through Penrith on the occasion of the FA cup tie between Carlisle and Preston on 15 February, 1964. The engine is in spotless crimson lake. In 1958, it was decided to repaint 20 Pacifics, based on the London Midland Region (16 'Coronations' and 4 'Princess Royals'), in crimson. Scottish Region examples remained in green./*P. J. Robinson*

Below: Also in spotless crimson lake, No 46251 *City of Nottingham* makes a superb sight as she speeds past the camera at the head of the 1.30pm Crewe–Carlisle goods train, at Winwick in January 1964./*J.R. Carter*

Above right: Also at Winwick, on a Crewe–Carlisle goods turn, No 46237 *City of Bristol* presents a more leisurely spectacle in May 1964. Increasing use of the class on such duties was the direct result of an influx of main line diesels to the Region./*J.R. Carter*

Right: A classic study of No 46256 *Sir William A. Stanier FRS* on shed, in crimson lake livery. This clearly shows the modified rear end of the last two Pacifics, with the reduced depth of the cab side sheets; cast steel trailing truck and modified frames. A diagonal yellow stripe on the cabside was added to the 19 members of the class still in service on 1 September, 1964 when they were prohibited south of Crewe due to height restrictions under overhead electric catenary. A last minute hope that some 'Coronations', could be transferred to the Waterloo–Bournemouth main-line of the SR was abandoned because of restricted clearances in the Southampton area. All remaining examples of this fine class were withdrawn from service in September 1964. The last to be in steam was very appropriately No 46256./*H. Wheeler*

4-6-0 Class 6P
(BR Power Class 7P)
Express Passenger Engines
Introduced: 1942
Total: 2
'Rebuilt Jubilee'

The hit-and-miss modifications made during attempts to improve the performance of the 5XP 'Jubilee' class 4-6-0s have already been mentioned. In 1937 it was proposed to rebuild some of the class with two outside cylinders only, but with a bigger boiler. The easement of weight restrictions on certain routes, however, permitted the retention of a 3-cylinder arrangement by the time it was decided to fit larger boilers to the class, in 1940. Even so the engine weight in working order was only increased by 2½ tons.

In early 1942 two engines were therefore given entirely new type 2A boilers and a new exhaust arrangement. In 1946 it was announced that the LMSR intended to extend this modification to the rest of the class, but the scheme never materialised and Nos 5735 *Comet* and 5736 *Phoenix,* were destined to remain the sole examples. In 1943 they were reclassified from 5XP to 6P, thereby making them the equivalent in power to the 'Royal Scot' class.

The principal chassis alterations were a rear extension of the frames and a new smokebox saddle. A double blastpipe and chimney were provided, and the top feed clacks were moved forward on to the first ring of the boiler barrel.

The new 2A boiler was identical to that later used on the 'Converted Royal Scot' class (Section 13) and had tubes 13ft long with a tube heating surface of 1,667sq ft, a firebox heating surface of 195sq ft, a total evaporative surface of 1,862sq ft, a grate area of 31.2sq ft, and a superheating surface of 357sq ft.

Later modifications to the boiler are detailed in the dimensional table below.

First of class withdrawn: 45736 (9/64)
Last of class withdrawn: 45735 (10/64)
None preserved

Top right: No 5735 *Comet,* in wartime plain black livery. Photographed at Camden./*P. Ransome-Wallis*

Centre right: In BR days the two 'Rebuilt Jubilees' received curved smoke deflectors similar to those of the 'Converted Royal Scots' and 'Rebuilt Patriots'. No 45736 *Phoenix* was photographed at Stafford in November 1959./*J.B. Bucknall*

Bottom right: Another view of No 45736 *Phoenix* taken at Newton Heath shed in September 1959, showing the standard BR AWS fitment below the buffer beam./*J.E. Wilkinson*

Heating surface, tubes
  Large and small: 1,656sq ft
  Firebox: 195sq ft
Total (evaporative): 1,851sq ft
Superheater: 367sq ft
  Superheater elements: 28
Combined heating surfaces: 2,218sq ft
Grate area: 31.25sq ft
Tractive effort (at 85 per cent BP): 29,590lb

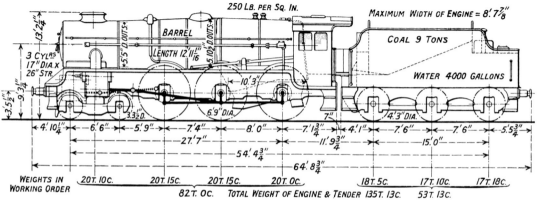

SECTION 13

4-6-0 Class 6P
(BR Power Class 7P)
Express Passenger Engines
Introduced: 1943
Total: 70
'Converted Royal Scot'

Known officially as the 'Converted Royal Scot' class, these engines were in effect almost complete rebuilds of the original Fowler design. Only the cab, the wheels, the tenders (of Stanier design in any case), and certain smaller features were retained from the Fowler engines. In fact their unofficial name of 'Rebuilt Scots' was a closer description! The original wheelbase dimensions were retained, but the maximum axle load was reduced by nearly half a ton, and the total locomotive weight was reduced by almost two tons.

Details of the type 2A boiler dimensions are given in the section on the 'Rebuilt Jubilees', but it is of interest to note that, compared to the unrebuilt parallel-boiler Fowler 'Royal Scots' the rebuilt version had over 200sq ft less evaporative heating surface. The tube proportions were, however, more favourable for good steaming. The firebox heating surface was 6sq ft greater; the grate area remained the same at 31.2sq ft; the superheating surface was reduced by 42sq ft. The working pressure remained at 250lb per sq in.

Authority was given in December 1942 for 20 'Royal Scot' conversions to be undertaken at Crewe. By this time engines had been in service for 12-15 years and were becoming due for new boilers and cylinders; there was also trouble from leaky smokeboxes. Candidates for conver-

sion were to be chosen on the state of their frames or cylinders, and the first to appear was No 6103 *Royal Scots Fusilier.* In June 1944, conversion of the remaining 50 was authorised, to take place over a period of seven years. Some engines had general repairs after 1943, without rebuilding, and it was not until 1955 that the last of the 70 locomotives in the class was rebuilt. This was No 46137 *The Prince of Wales Volunteers (South Lancashire).*

It is no exaggeration to claim that the 'Converted Royal Scots' were an outstanding successful class of locomotives in relation to their size. They put up some sparkling performances in everyday service and they gained an excellent reputation for steaming. One weakness was a tendency for rough riding to set in; this could be aptly described as wild, but safe!

Externally they had a pleasingly neat appearance, although this was later spoiled somewhat by the addition of smoke-deflectors. Apart from these, and alterations in livery, their appearance was virtually unchanged throughout their distinguished careers.

Right: 'Converted Royal Scot' No 6131 *The Royal Warwickshire Regiment* heads a down Manchester express near Tring. The locomotive is in postwar LMSR black livery, with maroon and straw lining-out./*E. Treacy*

Heating surface, tubes
  Large and small: 1,667sq ft
  Firebox: 195sq ft
Total (evaporative): 1,862sq ft
Superheater: 357sq ft
  Superheater elements: 28
Combined heating surfaces: 2,219sq ft
Grate area: 31.2sq ft
Tractive effort (at 85 per cent BP): 33,150lb

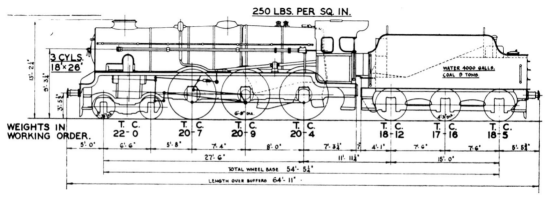

The main allocation of the class was always to the North Western main line, but the first few rebuilt were allocated to Leeds for through workings to Glasgow. In fact it was the ability to use them on that route, improving the motive power considerably, that allowed the work of conversion to be started in the war years. In their later days (circa 1957 onwards) they appeared on the Midland main line, and they also operated into Marylebone over the Great Central route.

First of class withdrawn: 46139 (1962)
Last of class withdrawn: 46115/28/40/52 (1965)
Examples preserved: 46100, 46115

Above: This shot of No 46127 *Old Contemptibles*, receiving the attention of a cleaner at Holyhead shed, also shows the postwar LMSR black livery with maroon and straw lining; a livery which seemed particularly suited to these engines./*E. Treacy*

Below: The two 'Converted Royal Scots' which featured in the 1948 Locomotive Exchanges were responsible for some impressive performances. To provide adequate water supply when operating on the Southern Region West of England main line, where no water troughs existed, No 46154 *The Hussar* was temporarily paired with an 8-wheel Austerity tender which was lettered LMS. She is seen passing Vauxhall with the 10.50am express to Plymouth on 7 June, 1948./*E.S.B. Elcombe*

Above right: A classic photograph of No 46162 *Queen's Westminster Rifleman,* the other 'Converted Scot' which featured in the 1948 Exchanges. Taken in Sonning Cutting, at the head of the up 8.30am Plymouth-Paddington express on 18 May, 1948./*M.W. Earley*

Right: Problems of drifting exhaust obscuring the driver's vision led to the adoption of small curved smoke-deflectors for the class. First to be fitted was No 6115 in August 1947. This illustration shows No 46105 *Cameron Highlander,* in clean BR green livery, at Tebay on the 4.20pm (Sundays only) Carlisle–Preston train; 15 May, 1955./*J.E. Wilkinson*

Above: Odd-man-out of the class was No 46106 *Gordon Highlander,* which received straight-sided smoke-deflectors somewhat similar to those employed on BR Standard locomotives. No 46106 is seen here (minus nameplates) working the southbound 4.45pm fish train from Perth; leaving Perth in June 1962./*W.J.V. Anderson*

Below: Commencing in 1962 the 'Converted Scots' were selected for scrapping as and when their condition warranted it. Those still in stock on 1 September, 1964 were henceforth prohibited from working south of Crewe, due to height restrictions for locomotives working under the energised 25kv catenary. A broad yellow diagonal stripe was painted on the cabsides to denote this restriction. No 46152 *The King's Dragoon Guardsman* is shown hauling the 3.40pm Bradford-Carlisle train out of Settle, on 3 April, 1965. It was withdrawn from service the very same month./*P.F. Claxton*

4-6-0 6P
(BR Power Class 7P)
Express Passenger Engines
Introduced: 1946
Total: 18
'Rebuilt Patriot'

'To meet postwar needs of accelerated express passenger services it has been decided to convert 18 parallel boiler 5X engines to take taper boilers . . . when requiring boiler renewals.' (LMSR Locomotive Committee minutes). This was the reasoning behind the approval granted in 1945 for the rebuilding of the 'Patriot' class, and while the first eight had only new front ends to the frames, the other ten had new frames with H. G. Ivatt's improvements. However, such was the degree of standardisation achieved by the LMSR that although not introduced until some two years after Stanier had ceased to have any direct personal influence upon LMSR locomotive affairs the 'Rebuilt Patriots' were entirely Stanier inspired. Fitted with the same superb Crewe 2A boiler that was applied to the 'Converted Royal Scots' and the 'Rebuilt Jubilees', the 'Rebuilt Patriots' were thus considered as equal 6P express passenger power. As rebuilt, their dimensions corresponded almost exactly with the two 'Rebuilt Jubilees' (see Section 12), and with a reduced cylinder diameter of 17in they had the identical tractive effort of 29,590lb, compared with the 33,150lb of the 'Converted Royal Scots'.

Of the total class of 52 'Patriots' only 18 were rebuilt and none of the first 12 of the class were included, as they had certain non-standard features. The rebuilding involved a new Stanier cab and tender as well as a new boiler. The tender was of standard 4,000 gallon, 9 ton capacity high curved side design.

Despite their lower tractive effort, the 'Rebuilt Patriots' took their place alongside the 'Converted Scots' in everyday service, and their performance was most satisfactory.

First of class withdrawn: 45514 (1961)
Last of class withdrawn: 45530 (1966)
None preserved

Below: In postwar LMSR black livery No 5530 *Sir Frank Ree* is seen in the 1947 official photograph./BR

Heating surface, tubes
   Large and small: 1,656sq ft
   Firebox: 195sq ft
Total (evaporative): 1,851sq ft
Superheater: 367sq ft
   Superheater elements: 28
Combined heating surfaces: 2,218sq ft
Grate area: 31.25sq ft
Tractive effort (at 85 per cent BP): 29,590lb

Top left: The 'Rebuilt Patriots' displayed the same handsome outline as the 'Converted Royal Scots', except that a Stanier cab replaced the original Fowler version. No 45535 *Sir Herbert Walker, KCB,* was photographed whilst painted in the experimental LNWR style lined black livery of early BR days. The top feed casing was of modified design, with more rounded appearance, introduced by Ivatt./*E. Treacy*

Left: Also in lined black livery, No 45522 *Prestatyn* is seen entering Liverpool Lime Street with a Whit Monday express in 1951./*K. Field*

Above: A fascinating comparison of the front ends of a 'Converted Royal Scot' and a 'Rebuilt Patriot', showing the subtle differences in appearance which existed. 'Rebuilt Patriot' No 45532 *Illustrious* was photographed alongside 'Converted Royal Scot' No 46143 *The South Staffordshire Regiment* on the arrival side at Euston./*P. Ransome-Wallis*

Below: Another shot of No 45532 *Illustrious,* this time on a more humble duty. She is seen climbing past Clifton, with the morning pick-up freight from Carlisle to Harrison's Sidings, Shap; May 1963. The 'Rebuilt Patriots' were fitted with curved smoke-deflectors of similar design to those applied to the Converted 'Royal Scots'; from 1948 onwards./*P.J. Robinson*

2-6-4T Class 4
Passenger Tank Engines
Introduced: 1945
Total: 277

The usefulness of the reliable Stanier 2-cylinder 2-6-4T design of 1935 (see page 70), was further extended by C. E. Fairburn. The 1940 building programme had included a further 45 Stanier 2-6-4Ts, but these were deferred due to wartime conditions and then 50 were ordered instead in the 1945 programme, to a modified design by Fairburn. The principal modification was a reduction of the coupled wheelbase from 16ft 6in to 15ft 4in, thereby enabling the engines to be used on 5-chain curves instead of the 6-chain limit of the original version. Coupled with a reduction of the overall weight in working order from 87.85 tons to 85.25 tons, this modification allowed an extension of their spheres of activity. Externally they differed but little from the earlier engines except at the front end, where the footplating was of shallow section and was cut away ahead of the cylinders; lighter section footplate steps were used.

The taper boiler had a working pressure of 200lb per sq in. The engines had self-cleaning smokeboxes, rocking grates and self-emptying ashpans.

The Fairburn version was widely distributed over the LMSR system and duties performed ranged from branch line and stopping trains to semi-fast express duties. They were used on the Southend line and in the Glasgow Suburban and Clyde Coast areas, as well as on outer-suburban duties from Euston and St Pancras. Other duties included banking and trip freight work, whilst on occasions they were called upon to act as pilots to ailing main-line express engines. After nationalisation further engines were built for service on the Southern, Eastern and North Eastern Regions pending completion of the design of R. A. Riddle's standard type of class 4 2-6-4T.

The engines were built as follows:

Nos 2673-2699	Derby	1945
Nos 2200-2217	Derby	1945
Nos 2218-2264	Derby	1946
Nos 2265-2299	Derby	1947

Right: Scottish enginemen in charge of the Fairburn 2-6-4Ts working on Glasgow suburban and Clyde Coast trains, kept their locomotives in immaculate condition. No 2242, with smokebox embellishments and with its plain black livery gleaming, was photographed on a Cathcart Circle suburban train leaving Glasgow Central on 24 April, 1948./*H.C. Casserley*

Heating surface, tubes
 Large and small: 1,226sq ft
 Firebox: 143sq ft
Total (evaporative): 1,369sq ft
Superheater: 230sq ft
 Superheater elements: 21
Combined heating surface: 1,599sq ft
Grate area: 26.7sq ft
Tractive effort (at 85 per cent BP): 24,670lb

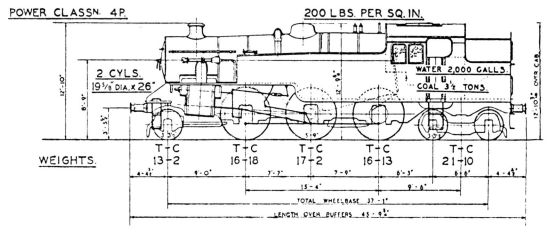

POWER CLASSN. 4P.   200 LBS. PER SQ. IN.

2 CYLS. 19⅝" DIA. x 26"

WATER 2,000 GALLS.
COAL 3½ TONS.

| WEIGHTS. | T–C 13–2 | T–C 16–18 | T–C 17–2 | T–C 16–13 | T–C 21–10 |

TOTAL WHEELBASE 37-1"
LENGTH OVER BUFFERS 45-9½"

Nos 2187-2189	Derby	1947
Nos 42147-42161	Derby	1948
Nos 42190-42199	Derby	1948
Nos 42162-42186	Derby	1949
Nos 42107-42132	Derby	1949
Nos 42133-42146	Derby	1950
Nos 42050-42053	Derby	1950

| Nos 42054-42065 | Derby | 1951 |
| Nos 42066-42106 | Brighton | 1950/51 |

First of class withdrawn: 42217 (1961)
Last of class withdrawn: 42072/3, 42085, 42093, (1967)
Examples preserved: 42073/85

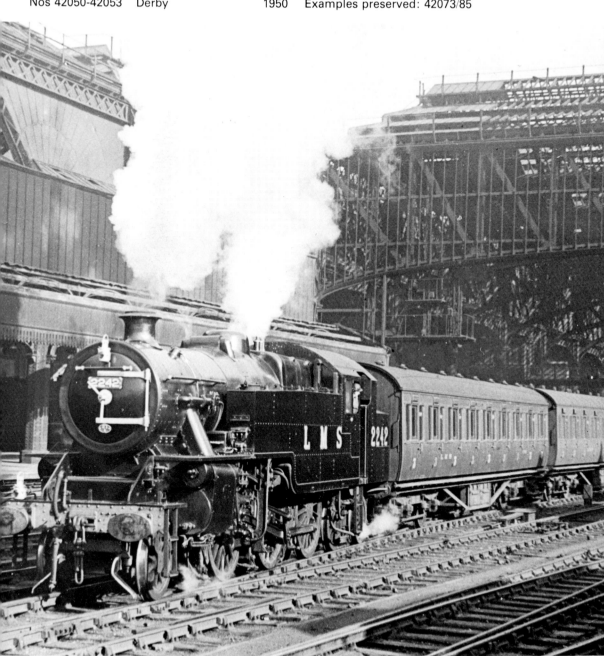

Top left: When new Nos 42198/9 ran trials on the Southern Region, to assess the suitability of the design for adoption as a replacement for the ageing fleet of locomotives working the steam-hauled trains on the Central Section. During the period of the 1948 Locomotive Exchanges, No 42199 ran a special trial train from Ashford (Kent) to Victoria, on 26 April 1948. A top speed of 85 mph was attained on this journey. No 42199 is seen leaving Ashford on this occasion./*P. Ransome-Wallis*

Centre left: The trials with Nos 42198/9 evidently proved satisfactory, as the decision was taken to construct 41 Fairburn 2-6-4Ts at Brighton Works for service on the Southern Region. Thus, for the second time in less than 10 years, Stanier locomotives were built at Brighton. The 2-6-4Ts were allocated to the SR Central Section, and gained a good reputation. No 42094 is illustrated working the 7.40am Birkenhead–Hastings through train, crossing Southerham Bridge, Lewes; on 11 June 1951./*S.C. Nash*

Bottom left: Brighton-built 2-6-4T No 42102 double heads SR 0-6-2T No 32585 on the 4.39pm to Tunbridge Wells West, seen leaving Eastbourne on 30 May, 1952. The Brighton-built Fairburn tanks were later drafted back to the London Midland, North Eastern and Scottish Regions, when new BR standard 2-6-4Ts took over their duties on the Southern./*S.C. Nash*

Above: No 42056, built at Derby, catches the evening sunlight as it leaves Glasgow St Enoch with a stopping train for the Ayrshire Coast./*D. Cross*

Below: Deputising for a failed 'Britannia' class Pacific; 2-6-4T No 42214 was photographed on Beattock Bank with a Ripon-Rutherglen troop special at Greskine, on 25 July, 1964. The train was banked from Greskine./*D. Cross*

Appendix 1

Named Locomotives

Showing all named Stanier locomotives taken over by British Railways, on 1 January 1948, and additional locomotives constructed under BR auspices.

Former LMSR locomotives are listed with the numbers carried prior to nationalisation. Locomotives constructed during nationalised days are shown with their BR number. All locomotives had 40,000 added to their existing running numbers, by BR. Thus for example, No 6220 became No 46220. For a while some locomotives carried the prefix **M** to their LMSR numbers, in 1948, prior to renumbering.

Power classifications were altered during BR days; the 6P 4-6-0s becoming 7P and the 7P 4-6-2s becoming 8P; the 5XPs became 6P.

4-6-0 Class 5 Mixed-Traffic
(see Section 4)

Only four engines of the class carried names in LMSR days, although No 5155 is sometimes quoted as *Queens Edinburgh.* Mystery surrounds this because no photographs have ever come to light showing the nameplates. Official LMSR correspondence dated 1938 listed it as named, and an 'on shed' check made in 1943 verified this. But it is a fact that none of the engine history cards relating to this engine record the name, although the other four are shown as named.

5154	Lanarkshire Yeomanry
5156	Ayrshire Yeomanry
5157	The Glasgow Highlander
5158	Glasgow Yeomanry

4-6-0 Class 6P (3-cyl)
Rebuilt by Ivatt to Stanier design
'Rebuilt Patriot'
(see Section 14)

45512	Bunsen
5514	Holyhead
5521	Rhyl
45522	Prestatyn
45523	Bangor
45525	Colwyn Bay
5526	Morecambe and Heysham
45527	Southport
5528	(1960: R.E.M.E.)

Below: Fitting the nameplate to de-streamlined 'Princess Coronation' Pacific No 46235 *City of Birmingham* in April 1946, with the engine finished in black livery. Note the City coat of arms attached to boiler side./*BR*

Right: 'Jubilee' class 4-6-0 No 5595 *Southern Rhodesia,* in LMSR crimson lake livery./*BR*

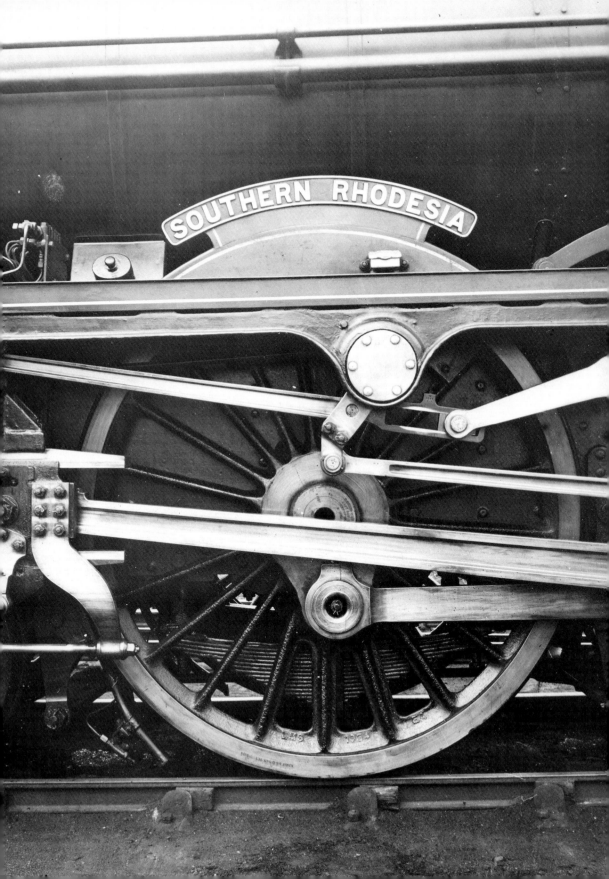

5529	(1949: Stephenson)	5574	India
5530	Sir Frank Ree	5575	Madras
5531	Sir Frederick Harrison	5576	Bombay
45532	Illustrious	5577	Bengal
45534	E. Tootal Broadhurst	5578	United Provinces
45535	Sir Herbert Walker, K.C.B.	5579	Punjab
45536	Private W. Wood, VC	5580	Burma
5540	Sir Robert Turnbull	5581	Bihar and Orissa
45545	(1948: Planet)	5582	Central Provinces
		5583	Assam

4-6-0 Class 5XP and 6P* (3-cyl)
'Jubilee'
(see Sections 3 and 12*)

5552	Silver Jubilee	5584	North West Frontier
†5553	Canada	5585	Hyderabad
5554	Ontario	5586	Mysore
5555	Quebec	5587	Baroda
5556	Nova Scotia	5588	Kashmir
5557	New Brunswick	5589	Gwalior
5558	Manitoba	5590	Travancore
5559	British Columbia	5591	Udaipur
5560	Prince Edward Island	5592	Indore
5561	Saskatchewan	5593	Kolhapur
5562	Alberta	5594	Bhopal
5563	Australia	5595	Southern Rhodesia
5564	New South Wales	†5596	Bahamas
5565	Victoria	5597	Barbados
5566	Queensland	5598	Basutoland
5567	South Australia	5599	Bechuanaland
5568	Western Australia	5600	Bermuda
5569	Tasmania	5601	British Guiana
5570	New Zealand	5602	British Honduras
5571	South Africa		
5572	Irish Free State (1938: Eire)		
5573	Newfoundland		

Below: 'Royal Scot' class 4-6-0 No 6170 *British Legion./BR*

Below right: 'Rebuilt Patriot' No 45529 *Stephenson* in 1948 black livery with LNWR-style lining-out./*BR.*

5603	Solomon Islands	5638	Zanzibar
5604	Ceylon	5639	Raleigh
5605	Cyprus	5640	Frobisher
5606	Falkland Islands	5641	Sandwich
5607	Fiji	5642	Boscawen
5608	Gibraltar	5643	Rodney
5609	Gilbert and Ellice Islands	5644	Howe
5610	Gold Coast (1958: Ghana)	5645	Collingwood
5611	Hong Kong	5646	Napier
5612	Jamaica	5647	Sturdee
5613	Kenya	5648	Wemyss
5614	Leewards Islands	5649	Hawkins
5615	Malay States	5650	Blake
5616	Malta (1943: Malta GC)	5651	Shovell
5617	Mauritius	5652	Hawke
5618	New Hebrides	5653	Barham
5619	Nigeria	5654	Hood
5620	North Borneo	5655	Keith
5621	Northern Rhodesia	5656	Cochrane
5622	Nyasaland	5657	Tyrwhitt
5623	Palestine	5658	Keyes
5624	St. Helena	5659	Drake
5625	Sarawak	5660	Rooke
5626	Seychelles	5661	Vernon
5627	Sierra Leone	5662	Kempenfelt
5628	Somaliland	5663	Jervis
5629	Straits Settlements	5664	Nelson
5630	Swaziland	5665	Lord Rutherford of Nelson
5631	Tanganyika	5666	Cornwallis
5632	Tonga	5667	Jellicoe
5633	Trans-Jordan (1946: Aden)	5668	Madden
5634	Trinidad	5669	Fisher
5635	Tobago	5670	Howard of Effingham
5636	Uganda	5671	Prince Rupert
5637	Windward Islands	5672	Anson

5673	Keppel	5729	Furious
5674	Duncan	5730	Ocean
5675	Hardy	5731	Perseverance
5676	Codrington	5732	Sanspareil
5677	Beatty	5733	Novelty
5678	De Robeck	5734	Meteor
5679	Armada	*5735	Comet
5680	Camperdown	*5736	Phoenix
5681	Aboukir	5737	Atlas
5682	Trafalgar	5738	Samson
5683	Hogue	5739	Ulster
†5684	Jutland	5740	Munster
5685	Barfleur	5741	Leinster
5686	St. Vincent	†5742	Connaught
5687	Neptune		
5688	Polyphemus		
5689	Ajax		
5690	Leander		
5691	Orion		
5692	Cyclops		
5693	Agamemnon		
5694	Bellerophon		
5695	Minotaur		
5696	Arethusa		
5697	Achilles		
5698	Mars		
5699	Galatea		

*Rebuilt 1942 with larger boilers and double chimneys. Reclassified 6P.
†Fitted with double chimneys at various times.

4-6-0 Class 6P (3-cyl)
'Converted Royal Scot'
(see Sections 10* and 13)

5700	Britannia (1951: Amethyst)	46100	Royal Scot
5701	Conqueror	6101	Royal Scots Grey
5702	Colossus	46102	Black Watch
5703	Thunderer	6103	Royal Scots Fusilier
5704	Leviathan	6104	Scottish Borderer
5705	Seahorse	46105	Cameron Highlander
5706	Express	46106	Gordon Highlander
5707	Valiant	46107	Argyll and Sutherland
5708	Resolution		Highlander
5709	Implacable	6108	Seaforth Highlander
5710	Irresistible	6109	Royal Engineer
5711	Courageous	46110	Grenadier Guardsman
5712	Victory	6111	Royal Fusilier
5713	Renown	6112	Sherwood Forester
5714	Revenge	46113	Cameronian
5715	Invincible	6114	Coldstream Guardsman
5716	Swiftsure	6115	Scots Guardsman
5717	Dauntless	6116	Irish Guardsman
5718	Dreadnought	6117	Welsh Guardsman
5719	Glorious	6118	Royal Welch Fusilier
5720	Indomitable	6119	Lancashire Fusilier
5721	Impregnable	6120	Royal Inniskilling Fusilier
†5722	Defence	6121	Highland Light Infantry, City of Glasgow Regiment, (formerly H.L.I.)
5723	Fearless	6122	Royal Ulster Rifleman
5724	Warspite	46123	Royal Irish Fusilier
5725	Repulse	6124	London Scottish
5726	Vindictive	6125	3rd Carabinier
5727	Inflexible	6126	Royal Army Service Corps
5728	Defiance	6127	Old Contemptibles
		6128	The Lovat Scouts
		6129	The Scottish Horse

Introduced 1935. Stanier taper-boiler rebuild of experimental high-pressure compound locomotive No 6399 Fury.

Below: Sir William A. Stanier at the controls of 'Princess Coronation' Pacific No 6256 on the occasion of the naming ceremony in his honour; 17 December, 1947. Standing on the footplate is Sir Robert Burrows, LMSR Chairman./BR

4-6-2 Class 7P (4-cyl)
'Princess Royal'
(see Sections 1 and 6*)

6200	The Princess Royal
6201	Princess Elizabeth
*6202	(1952: Princess Anne)
6203	Princess Margaret Rose
6204	Princess Louise
6205	Princess Victoria
6206	Princess Marie Louise
6207	Princess Arthur of Connaught
6208	Princess Helena Victoria
6209	Princess Beatrice
6210	Lady Patricia
6211	Queen Maud
6212	Duchess of Kent

*Introduced 1935. Experimental turbine-driven locomotive (the 'Turbomotive'). Rebuilt 1952 as conventional 4-cyl Pacific.

4-6-2 Class 7P (4-cyl)
'Princess Coronation' (or 'Duchess')
(see Section 11)

6220	Coronation
6221	Queen Elizabeth
6222	Queen Mary
6223	Princess Alice
6224	Princess Alexandra
6225	Duchess of Gloucester
6226	Duchess of Norfolk
6227	Duchess of Devonshire
6228	Duchess of Rutland
6229	Duchess of Hamilton
6230	Duchess of Buccleuch
6231	Duchess of Atholl
6232	Duchess of Montrose
6233	Duchess of Sutherland
6234	Duchess of Abercorn
6235	City of Birmingham
6236	City of Bradford
6237	City of Bristol
6238	City of Carlisle
6239	City of Chester
6240	City of Coventry
6241	City of Edinburgh
6242	City of Glasgow
6243	City of Lancaster
6244	King George VI (formerly City of Leeds)
6245	City of London
6246	City of Manchester
6247	City of Liverpool
6248	City of Leeds
6249	City of Sheffield

6250	City of Lichfield
6251	City of Nottingham
6252	City of Leicester
6253	City of St. Albans
6254	City of Stoke-on-Trent
6255	City of Hereford
†6256	Sir William A. Stanier, F.R.S
†46257	City of Salford

†Introduced 1947. Ivatt development with roller bearings and detail alterations.

2-8-0 Class 8F (2-cyl)
War Department – Middle East Forces
(see Section 7)
The following were named circa 1952:

70320	Lt W. O. Lennox VC
70373	C/Sgt. H. McDonald VC
70387	Cpl W. J. Lendrim VC
70395	Capt H. G. Elphinstone VC
70501	Spr John Perie VC
70516	Cpl J. Ross VC
70574	Cpl Leitcher VC
70593	Lt Gramham VC

Each nameplate had the added inscription ROYAL ENGINEERS placed below the name and the regimental badge above. All those named had won their Victoria Crosses in the Crimean War and there was a commemorative plaque in the cab, describing the circumstances of the award. WD No 421 was named *Wolfe* when used as an instructional locomotive at Longmoor in 1941. The post-1952 WD numbers were 501/514/503/6/7/9/510/1/3.

Longmoor Military Railway (circa 1954-5).
WD No 511	Sgt J. Smith VC Bengal Sappers & Miners

Diesel Shunting Locomotives
(see page 125 for details of wheel arrangement, etc.)
Some former LMSR diesel shunters were named whilst in War Department service, as follows:

70270	Bari
70271	Bari (transferred from 70270)

Top right: The nameplate and motion of 'Converted Royal Scot' class 4-6-0 No 46127 *Old Contemptibles* receives an extra polish at Holyhead shed, as the engine waits to head the 'Irish Mail'./*E. Treacy*

Right: War Department Stanier 2-8-0 No 70320 carrying the name *Lt. W.O. Lennox VC,* seen awaiting repair at Suez in 1951./*BR*

70272	Chittagong (*later* Basra)
70213	(ex-7059)Old Joe
70214	(ex-7061)Pluto
70215	(ex-7062)Flying Scotsman*
70217	(ex-7064)Ubique

Nos 70270-2 were on the Longmoor Military Railways and Nos 70213/4/7 were sent to Belgium.

70215 later became WD882.

Appendix 2

Preserved Locomotives

When I first sat down to write this book in August 1968, the boilers of the last steam locomotives to run in BR ownership (other than the narrow-gauge Vale of Rheidol tanks) were still cooling-down. Like thousands of others I made my pilgrimage to Ais Gill and beyond to witness the day's events when, on Sunday 11 August 1968 the special last train was run, (see picture on page 18). Perhaps it was no coincidence that examples of Stanier's 'Black Fives' played an important part in this melancholy celebration. For after all, the 'Black Fives' were the epitome of his work and of the rugged British steam engine in all its basic simplicity. They seemed too good to die, and it was heartening news indeed that so many examples of the class, and of other Stanier types, had been earmarked by various people for future preservation.

Then came that dreadful period when BR management turned its back upon the steam locomotive, and tried hard to convince itself and the public that steam was *dead*. A total ban on steam running on BR tracks was only excelled in its stupidity by a total ban upon any mention of the word! But steam refused to die, and thanks to the countless rail enthusiasts and their efforts, both physical and financial, and to a more enlightened attitude within the railways hierarchy, the picture today is a very encouraging one indeed.

There are 28 Stanier locomotives in preserved state and a possibility even now that one or two more may be resurrected from the Barry graveyard. In the list that follows I have indicated those that were in working order, and those passed for running on BR, as at May 1980, but it must be emphasised that the picture is constantly changing. Some engines are still undergoing overhaul and some which have been in steam now await repair or overhaul. Details of ownership and liveries are also given as far as possible, but further information from readers would be welcomed by the author, % Ian Allan Ltd. Space does not permit me to reproduce pictures of all the preserved Stanier locos, but a representative selection accompanies this appendix.

Right: Close-up of No 6201 *Princess Elizabeth* at Tyseley in May 1970./*J.H. Cooper-Smith*

No	Name	Location	Owner	Livery
6201 *†	Princess Elizabeth	Bulmer's Rly Centre, Hereford.	Princess Elizabeth Locomotive Society	LMSR crimson lake
6203	Princess Margaret Rose	Midland Rly Centre, Butterley	Butlins Ltd (formerly on display at Pwllheli)	LMSR crimsom lake
46229 *†	Duchess of Hamilton	National Rly Museum, York.	Butlins Ltd. (formerly on display at Minehead)	BR crimson lake
6233 *	Duchess of Sutherland	Bressingham Steam Museum, Diss, Norfolk.	Butlins Ltd (formerly on display at Heads of Ayr)	LMSR crimson lake
46235 *	City of Birmingham	Museum of Science & Ind Newhall st, Birmingham.	City of Birmingham (Donated by BR and placed on site in May 1966 Museum extension built around locomotive.)	BR green
6100 *	Royal Scot	Bressingham Steam Museum, Diss, Norfolk.	Butlins Ltd. (Formerly on display at Skegness)	LMSR crimson lake (incorrect shading to letters & figures)
6115 *	Scots Guardsman	Dinting Rly Centre, Glossop, Derbyshire.		LMSR 1946 black straw & maroon lining
5593 *†	Kolhapur	Birmingham Rly Museum, Tyseley, Birmingham.		LMSR crimson lake
5596	Bahamas	Dinting Rly Centre, Glossop, Derbyshire.		LMSR crimson lake
5690 *	Leander	Steamtown, Carnforth.	Leander Locomotive Ltd.	LMSR crimson lake
45699	Galatea	Steamtown, Carnforth.	Leander Locomotive Ltd.	
4767 *†	George Stephenson	North Yorkshire Moors Rly		LMSR 1946 black
44806	Magpie	Steamport, Southport		green
44871 *†	Sovereign	Steamtown, Carnforth.		BR black, lined.
44932 *		Steamtown, Carnforth		green
5000 *†		Severn Valley Rly.	National Rly Museum	LMSR black lined red.
5025 *†		Strathspey Rly		LMSR black lined red.
45110 *	R.A.F Biggin Hill	Severn Valley Rly		BR black, lined
45212		Keighley & Worth Valley Rly		BR black, lined first emblem
5231	3rd (Volunteer) Battalion The Worcestershire and Sherwood Foresters Regiment	Great Central Rly		LMSR black, lined
5305 *†		Hull Dairy Coates	Humberside Locomotive Preservation Group	LMSR black, lined 1936 block figures
45379		Bristol Suburban Rly		
45407 *†		Steamtown, Carnforth.		BR black, lined.
5428	Eric Treacy	North Yorkshire Moors Rly		LMSR black, lined block letters
48151				
8233 *	(former BR number 48773 (former WD number 307)	Severn Valley Rly	The Stanier 8F Locomotive Society	LMSR black, unlined
8431		Keighley & Worth Valley Rly		LMSR black, unlined
48518		Peak Railway Society, Buxton		
2968		Severn Valley Rly.	The Stanier Mogul Fund	
2500 *		Bressingham Steam Museum, Diss, Norfolk.	National Rly Museum	LMSR black, lined.

*Indicates that the engine is in working order.
†Indicates that the engine is passed for running on BR.
Names in italics indicate naming after purchase from BR.

Above: A study of No 6203 *Princess Margaret Rose* stored at Derby in 1975 after leaving Butlins at Pwllheli, North Wales, on route to the Midland Railway Centre./*Midland Society*

Below: 'Princess Coronation' or 'Duchess' class No 6233 *Duchess of Sutherland* displays the sleek lines of Stanier's non-streamlined Pacifics, amidst the sylvan setting of Alan Bloom's nursery gardens at Bressingham, in July 1974./ *J. Edgington*

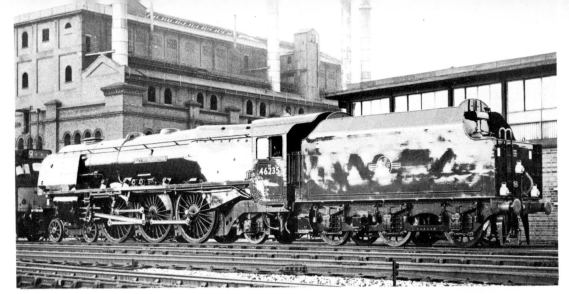

Top left: No 46235 *City of Birmingham* restored to BR green livery and seen at Birmingham prior to completion of the Museum extension, in May 1966./*J.W. Ellson*

Left: 'Jubilee' class No 5690 *Leander* caught in a striking camera angle at Wennington in October 1979./*R. Payne*

Above: 'Converted Royal Scot' No 6100 *Royal Scot* at Bressingham in May 1973. Restored to an incorrect livery of crimson lake, which it never carried after conversion by Stanier./*J. Edgington*

Below: The correct postwar livery of black with maroon and straw lining is carried by 'Converted Royal Scot' No 6115 *Scots Guardsman,* seen here at Dinting in June 1979./*J. Edgington*

Above left: The unique Stephenson valve geared 'Black Five' is amongst the members of the class to have been preserved. Now named *George Stephenson,* and with single chimney, No 4767 is seen on a Pickering–Grosmount train in May 1977./*David Eatwell*

Left: 'Black Five' No 5305 makes haste south of York with a BR special in July 1978./*R.E.B. Siviter*

Above: Now named *Eric Treacy,* 'Black Five' No 5428 is seen at Tyseley in May 1969./*J.W. Ellson*

Right: Close-up of Stanier 8F No 8233 (formerly BR 48773) at Tyseley in May 1970; (see also page 68)./*J.H. Cooper-Smith*

Above: Restored 8F No 8431 (with WR-type ejector pipe on boiler side) pauses during a spell of duty on the Keighley and Worth Valley line./*J. Edgington*

Left: A reminder of the hard work that goes into locomotive restoration. Saved from the scrapyard torch, Stanier Mogul No 42968 gets the benefit of dedicated enthusiasm, at Bridgnorth in June 1977./*J. Edgington*

Above right: Double-chimney 'Jubilee' No 5596 seen nearing All Stretton with a Manchester–Newport special in October 1972./*T. Stephens*

Right: Typical scene at an open day, as 'Jubilee' No 5593 *Kolhapur* gathers the crowds at Tyseley in May 1969./ *D. Birch*

Above: 'Black Five' No 44806 *Magpie* keeps some odd company outside 'Steamport', Southport in March 1975./ *L. Wheelwright*

Below: Another of the preserved 'Black Fives' No 45110 (since named *RAF Biggin Hill*) seen heading the 4pm Bridgnorth, on the Severn Valley Railway; September 1970./*W.N. Lockett*

Appendix 3

Diesel Shunting Locomotives

Of the four main line railways it was the LMSR that took the greatest steps in developing diesel shunting locomotives, and (after Stanier's time) diesel main line locomotives. When Stanier arrived work was in hand with the conversion of a former Midland 0-6-0T No 1831 into a diesel hydraulic shunter, and this was completed late in 1932. It was far from successful, but a Hunslet mechanical shunter which worked at Leeds during 1932 surpassed all expectations, so in January 1933 it was agreed to purchase ten machines of similar size and a larger diesel electric locomotive. The shunters supplied are shown in the table at the foot of the page.

No 7051 was the locomotive that had been on trial in 1932. It will be seen that eight only of the small locomotives were supplied. Not to be outdone the steam supporters succeeded in using the authority to order two Sentinel-Doble oil fired compound engines, but only one, No 7192 was ever completed and this was delivered in 1934. It had the distinction of being the last steam shunting engine obtained by the LMSR, more than 20 years before British Railways put into service its last steam shunter! The performance varied considerably, Nos 7055-7 being the least satisfactory. During the war years five passed into Government use and one, No 7057 returned to Ireland. No 7058 last until just after nationalisation.

As a consequence of C. E. Fairburn taking charge of electrical matters it was the larger 350hp six-coupled type with electric transmission that later found favour with the LMSR. Two types were ordered in the 1935 Programme:

Nos 7059-68   Armstrong Whitworth   1936
(Max speed 20mph)

Nos 7069-78   Hawthorn Leslie   1936
(Max speed 30mph)
No 7079*   Hawthorn Leslie   1934
(Max Speed 35mph)

No 7079 was a demonstrator and was taken into LMSR stock in 1936. Originally it was rated at 300hp but was modified to meet LMSR requirements. Nos 7074/6/9 became BR Nos 12000-2.

The two types differed radically in the layout of the transmission; Nos 7059-68 had a single frame mounted motor with a jackshaft drive and the others had two naturally ventilated single reduction nose suspended motors and they suffered from overheating of the motors when hump shunting. So the jackshaft drive was selected for further construction and English Electric got the orders for the engines and electrical equipment, the locomotives being erected at Derby:

Nos 7080-9   1939   (BR Nos 12003-12)
Nos 7090-9   1940   (BR Nos 12013-22)
Nos 7100-9   1941
Nos 7110-9   1942   (BR Nos 12023-32)

Following the outbreak of war all the Armstrong Whitworth locomotives passed into War Department hands, several being sent overseas and eight of the 11 Hawthorn Leslie shunters were sent to France, all being lost. Nos 7100-15 went direct into WD service as Nos 49-64, but the LMSR was in desperate need of shunting power so the last six were returned very quickly.

The final development of the 350hp shunter, indeed to its current form, occurred in 1940 when No 7074 was modified; the motors were altered to have a double reduction gearing and forced ventilation, a change which overcame the overheating problems and made them eminently suitable for hump shunting, while the reduction to 20mph of the maximum speed was no

No 7050	0-4-0DM	160hp	English Electric/Drewry	1934
Nos 7051-3*	0-6-0DM	150hp	Hunslet	1932-4
No 7054	0-6-0DM	180hp	Hunslet	1934
Nos 7055/6	0-6-0DM	150hp	Hudswell Clarke	1934-5
No 7057	0-6-0DM	175hp	Harland & Wolfe	1935
No 7058*	0-6-0DE	250hp	Armstrong Whitworth	1934

Supplied as Nos 7401-3 and 7408 (All were to have been Nos 7400-8).

impediment. Despite wartime conditions the LMSR optimistically ordered 100 new locomotives of this revised type in December 1940, but of course delays in manufacturing programmes inhibited construction, although some work was done by English Electric. The WD demanded more diesel power and 40 were to have been built at Derby, to be WD Nos 260-99; thus it came about that a Stanier design came to be ordered for use elsewhere than on the LMSR! However only 14 went to the WD, the LMSR taking six and the rest were cancelled. For postwar construction the LMSR and British Railways ordered a further 30 and 70 respectively:

WD Nos 260-73	1944-5	Derby
Nos 7120-5*	1945	Derby
Nos 7126-31†	1947-8	Derby
Nos 12045-68‡	1948-50	Derby
Nos 12069-12102	1950-2	Derby
Nos 12103-38**	1952-3	Darlington

*Ordered as WD Nos 274-9 and became BR Nos 12033-8
†Became BR Nos 12039-44
‡Ordered as LMSR Nos 7132-55.
**Ordered by British Railways for use on E/NE Regions.

Left: Publicity picture of August 1936, showing a line-up of diesel shunters at Crewe with No 7072 in the foreground./*Ian Allan Library*

Below: Derby-built jackshaft drive shunter No 7080, with English Electric equipment, delivered in 1939./*BR*

Bottom: In BR green livery and with warning end paint scheme No 12009 (ex-LMS 7086) was photographed at Newton Heath in May 1960./*J.E. Wilkinson*

This picture: Memories of Stanier steam classically-portrayed at Heaton Mersey shed on April 19, 1968 as Class 8F 2-8-0s Nos 48322 and 48551 take a rest from duty; just three weeks before closure of the shed./*John A.M. Vaughan*